PAMELA'S PATTERNS

ISBN:9781546502074

Other Books by Pamela Hastings Include:

Doll Making as a Transformative Process

Paper Doll Inspiration

Designing a Doll and Making Faces

A Moment of Pure Joy on an Ordinary Day

Hot Flash Women

Available as e-Books:

Doll Making as a Transformative Process

Altered Books

Fabric Journals

Icons and Angels

Ancestor Making

And Many More Art and Making Books to Come!

I've been making dolls since I was five. When I was in Junior High School I started with the Women's Day Christmas doll patterns, which evolved into making Edith Flack Ackley costume dolls, then dolls to represent my fellow Community Theater Characters. I was also learning to sew clothes for myself, which taught me how to cut and shape flat fabric to make 3-D forms.

I married the day I graduated from college, silly me, and my husband and I started doing outdoor craft fairs in Boston and dipping candles in our apartment. I resumed my doll making career with soft toys, it was still the Sixties. I saw an exhibit of Lenore Davis' Art Dolls, and figured out that I could use acrylic paints on muslin to create more colors and effects.

We moved to an old schoolhouse in the Northeast Kingdom of Vermont, and a life-long passion for doll making bloomed. The world was ready for Art Dolls, I discovered a skill for 3D design, and the Rest is History.

Pieced body, painted wooden spoon for head...Let your imagination know no bounds!

Happy Icon, pieced with beads

Table of Contents

Queen of the May Embraces her Darker Self
Piecing with Ivory faces, charms, feathers

INTRODUCTION 1

I have been making dolls since 1952, which means a large number of dolls. I've taught doll making and designed patterns....I seem to have a facility for three-dimensional pattern design, although not for making clothes that fit me. I started doll making by using other people's patterns--Woman's Day, the magazine, published doll patterns for Christmas in the Sixties, and I started with altering those and gradually branched out to design my own patterns.

How do I take a piece of flat fabric and transform it into a three-dimensional doll? If you have been asking yourself this question, this is the book for you.

I encourage you to use these patterns as a jumping off point to develop your own designs. Copy the pattern, enlarge it to make stitching more comfortable, and use a glue stick to attach it to poster board for stiffness. Use an extra fine point sharpie to trace around the pattern piece onto the back side of your fabric. For best results use a finely-woven cotton, adding a 1/8" seam allowance outside the drawn lines. For most of the dolls, sew two pieces with right sides together, using a short stitch length, stitching right on top of the drawn line. Most pattern pieces will require leaving an opening one to one and a half inches long on a straight side for turning and stuffing. The tool I use for that task is a wooden chop stick with the end sharpened in a pencil sharpener, then sanded smooth. The patterns have been sized to fit on the pages, so you may want to scan and enlarge, trying to enlarge all parts of the patterns the same amount. The larger body parts will be much easier to sew and turn, especially if you are a beginning seamstress.

Use a ladder stitch (p75) to close the opening after turning and stuffing or to attach body parts as invisibly as possible. Try to match the thread to your fabric...although when I was doing production doll sewing, I used white or natural-colored thread on top and black in the bobbin, so the two colors of thread would blend with most fabrics without having to change thread and bobbins frequently. When working with silk or other stretchy fabric, back the piece with light shirt-weight iron-on interfacing before drawing and cutting out the pattern piece.

I love piecing to use up small beautiful bits of fabric. I like to combine lots of prints and colors. If you feel insecure about your color choices, pick a multicolored small print for a key segment of the doll, then match the other fabrics to that color choice.

Have fun, experiment, adapt the patterns for your own needs, email me photos of what you do. I'm trying to keep this book as much in black and white as I can, to keep your price down. You may be interested in seeing more of my dolls in color in the gallery on my web site www.pamelahastings.com, my blog: www.pamelabythesea.wordpress.com or in my other books, available at www.healingandtransformativedolls.com or on Amazon.

The pattern for White Angels is on page 28. Once you have followed enough patterns, you can start to adapt them to your own designs--that's how I learned. Now I get so inspired looking at Pinterest, I keep pieces of paper by my computer to sketch out additional designs. I must force myself to stop adding yet more patterns to this book. My Word Press blog is the next project, so eventually you'll find more new patterns there.

SIMPLE FORMS: ICONS AND ANGELS 2

White Angels: Very Simple Icon body pattern, made with a selection of white-on-white printed cotton. The faces are approximately 1.5" square high-contrast faces from Teesha Moore printed onto cotton fabric. Feet are pearl and crystal beads. The hand and arm charms are pewter, from Art Girlz. A white one-piece wing, quilted with white thread, fuzzy white yarn hair and hanging loops, hearts and pearl and crystal beads. A grouping, especially in a common color way is very effective.

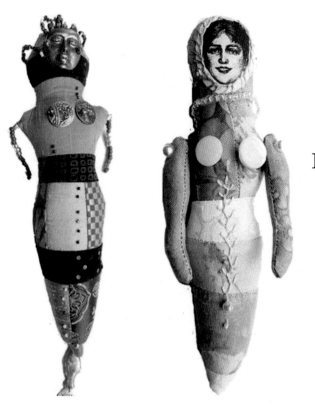

Icons are simple forms, but the simpler the form, the more flexible for expressing a wide range of intentions. Experiment with altering the basic shapes below. Attach different types of arms and legs or use charms or beads.

Icons

Use the Simple Icon pattern to make all types, including Antique Icons. Use a printed face or a charm face, sew and stuff arms and legs, with size adjusted to the size of the body or use charms or a string of beads for the limbs. Decorate with embroidery, beads, or create your own fancy hats with feathers.

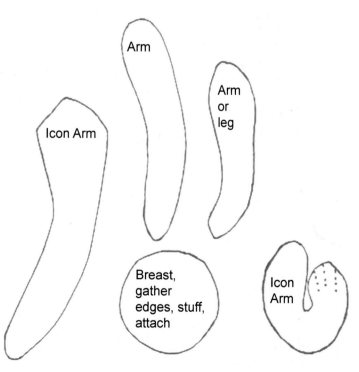

Arm

Arm or leg

Icon Arm

Breast, gather edges, stuff, attach

Icon Arm

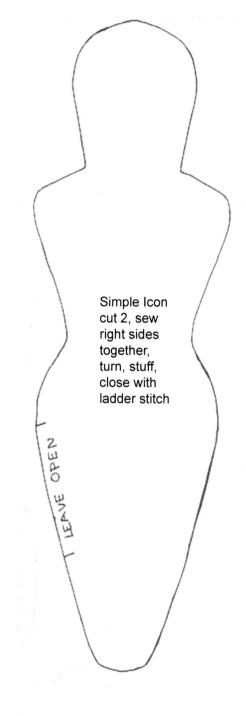

Simple Icon cut 2, sew right sides together, turn, stuff, close with ladder stitch

LEAVE OPEN

There are endless possibilities with slight variations in shape/color/decoration.

You can make icons symmetrical by folding the shape in half and cutting both sides at the same time. Keep the outline fairly simple...be inspired by ancient icons...lots of examples on Pinterest.

Icons make great gifts. They can be adapted to any occasion or personal taste by the fabric in which they are made or the way they are embellished. Copy and enlarge or decrease the size of this pattern to suit your fancy. Piece (sew small bits of fabric together) a shape large enough to make this icon--you'll need two pieces 7" tall by 3" wide. Sew the outside seam on the traced line with small stitches, then sew another line of stitching just outside the first.

I made a special icon when my brother, David, got his studio space. The artistical-ly-patterned fabric adds to the look of complexity, even though the body shape is very simple.

I used red wire stitched to the top of the head for hair, a very simple eye-brow/nose embroidered to suggest a face, and Art, Create, Joy embroidered on the chest. A red rubber ring sewn to the back for hanging.

Studio Icon

One-Armed Icon

Let go of your preconceived notions about what a doll should look like. A human figure is recognizable in lots of different configurations. I keep sketching materials near each place where I sit, so I can jot down ideas. With the advent of computers, I can scan even the roughest sketch and enlarge the parts into pattern pieces.

These quirky little dolls allow me to use a variety of fabrics in unusual combinations, attaching body parts with beads, using beads for hair, making the goldfish in the body stand out with a line of beading and embroidery for the simplest suggestion of features. You could embroider an encouraging phrase on the body to create a gift, or dedicate this doll to an intention.

Try enlarging or decreasing the size of the pattern for different effects. If only one arm bothers you, make two.

Add the limbs in different places or change their shapes.
Make the hair with yarn or strings of beads.

Use a photo-transfer sewn on, or attached with beads for a face.
The Possibilities are Endless!

One-Armed Icon Pattern

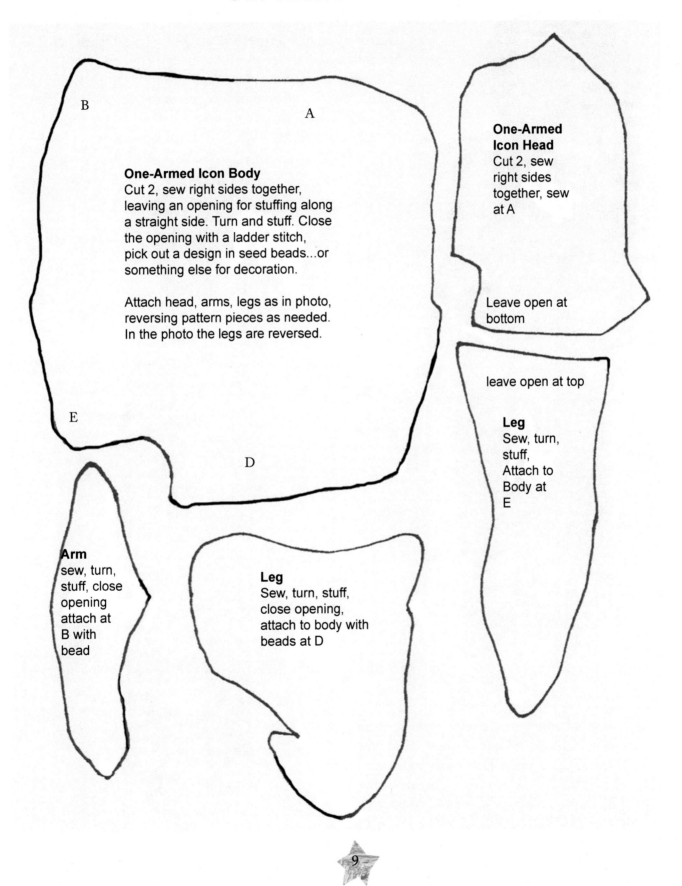

B

A

One-Armed Icon Body
Cut 2, sew right sides together, leaving an opening for stuffing along a straight side. Turn and stuff. Close the opening with a ladder stitch, pick out a design in seed beads...or something else for decoration.

Attach head, arms, legs as in photo, reversing pattern pieces as needed. In the photo the legs are reversed.

One-Armed Icon Head
Cut 2, sew right sides together, sew at A

Leave open at bottom

leave open at top

Leg
Sew, turn, stuff, Attach to Body at E

E

D

Arm
sew, turn, stuff, close opening attach at B with bead

Leg
Sew, turn, stuff, close opening, attach to body with beads at D

Ancestor and Portrait Icons

The doll on the left, Heroine Doll pattern, uses my face as a prolific artist/teenager. The head is joined to the shoulder with less of an indent than the pattern. Lots of beads, and a phrase embroidered with combined colors of floss... and a mis-spelling of WINNS...I have always thought that poor spelling is a sign of high intelligence.

The doll on the right is my great grandmother... these simple bodies, paired with faces printed on cloth (see resources section at the back) make wonderful gifts or intentions for living your own life as the Heroine of your story. Small variations in color, texture, shape, and embellishment can create a Very Different effect!

10

Ancestor and Portrait
Icons

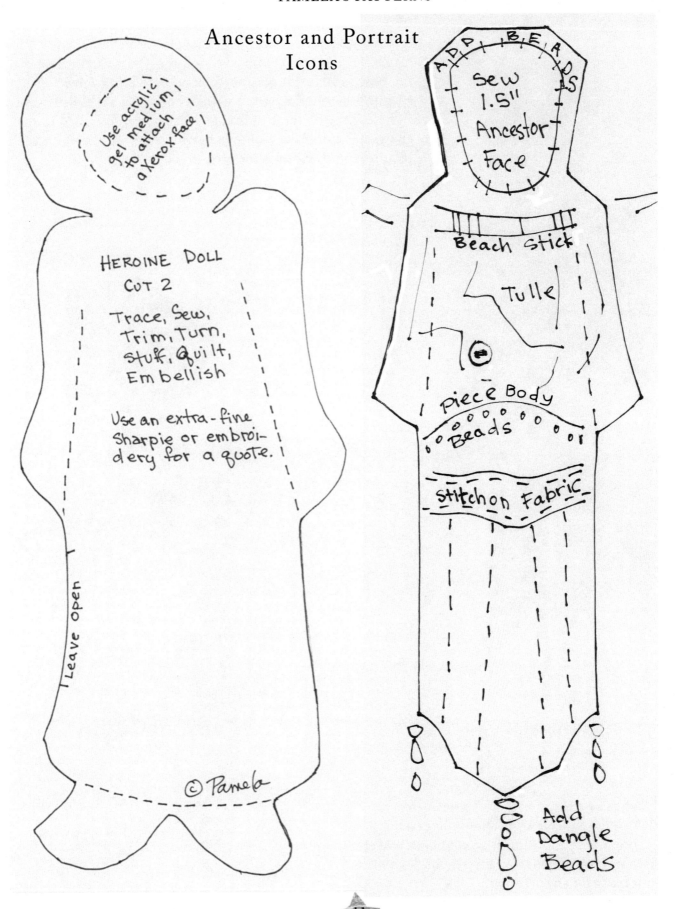

Use acrylic gel medium to attach a Xerox face

HEROINE DOLL
CUT 2

Trace, Sew, Trim, Turn, Stuff, Quilt, Embellish

Use an extra-fine Sharpie or embroidery for a quote.

Leave open

© Pamela

ADD BEADS

Sew 1.5" Ancestor Face

Beach Stick

Tulle

Piece Body

Beads

Stitch on Fabric

Add Dangle Beads

Icon with Cord: I draw a lot of inspiration from ancient forms, such as this icon using a running stitch to outline the nose (stitch side to side, picking up a bit of fabric and stuffing). A running stitch with beads picks out the arms, and I used two pieces of orange leather cord couched to the chest, and half-sphere orange beads held onto the chest with sequins and tiny beads for breasts.

Icon with Cord

Imp

I love using my scraps to sew up a bunch of these little guys, experimenting with new body shapes. and embellishment Then I have a basket of things to work on while I watch movies, plus gifts ready for any occasion.

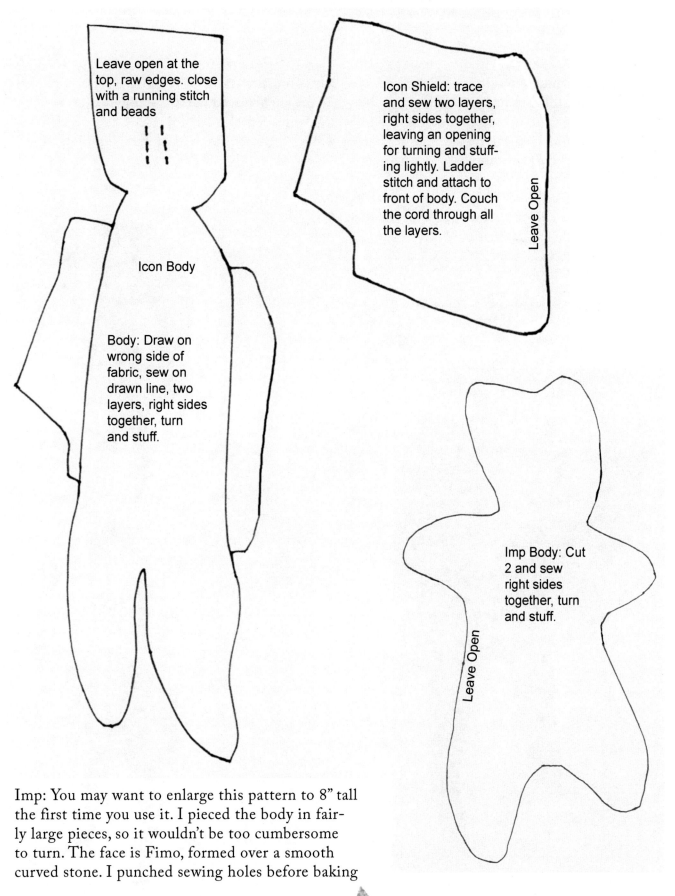

Leave open at the top, raw edges. close with a running stitch and beads

Icon Body

Icon Shield: trace and sew two layers, right sides together, leaving an opening for turning and stuffing lightly. Ladder stitch and attach to front of body. Couch the cord through all the layers.

Leave Open

Body: Draw on wrong side of fabric, sew on drawn line, two layers, right sides together, turn and stuff.

Imp Body: Cut 2 and sew right sides together, turn and stuff.

Leave Open

Imp: You may want to enlarge this pattern to 8" tall the first time you use it. I pieced the body in fairly large pieces, so it wouldn't be too cumbersome to turn. The face is Fimo, formed over a smooth curved stone. I punched sewing holes before baking

Sprite

When transforming oneself, it's helpful to have a focus for intentions...the Sprite carries a pocket
full of fortunes--I love saving these, especially when I want them to pertain to my future.
She makes a fun little companion, or a way to send best wishes to a friend.
The doll looks more complicated than it actually is: just 5 two-piece pattern parts, and lots of
opportunity for embellishment.

You may sew the pocket to the body by machine before sewing
the front to the back or use a hand blanket stitch
to sew the pocket to the stuffed body.

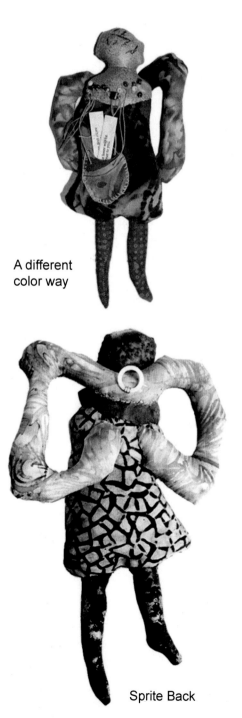

A different
color way

Sprite Back

Sprite Pattern

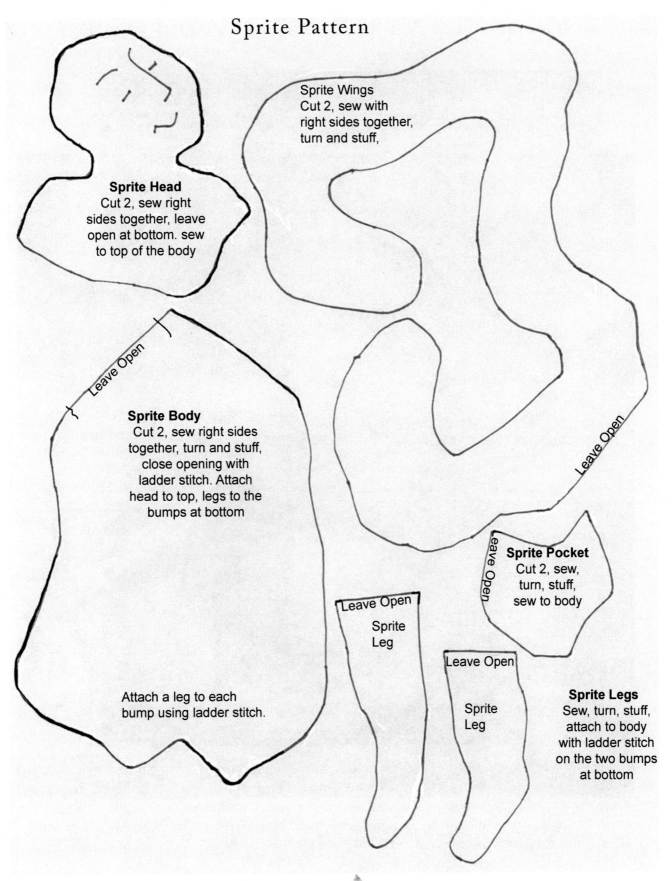

Sprite Head
Cut 2, sew right sides together, leave open at bottom. sew to top of the body

Sprite Wings
Cut 2, sew with right sides together, turn and stuff,

Leave Open

Sprite Body
Cut 2, sew right sides together, turn and stuff, close opening with ladder stitch. Attach head to top, legs to the bumps at bottom

Leave Open

Sprite Pocket
Cut 2, sew, turn, stuff, sew to body

Leave Open
Sprite Leg

Leave Open
Sprite Leg

Sprite Legs
Sew, turn, stuff, attach to body with ladder stitch on the two bumps at bottom

Attach a leg to each bump using ladder stitch.

DOLL MAKING AS A TRANSFORMATIVE PROCESS   3

I am probably best known for my work with doll making as a tool for life-change. I've taught my online classes to students all over the world and some art therapy programs in the US and Australia use my book, Doll Making as a Transformative Process, available for printing on demand at Amazon. I'm including some of the patterns from that book here...they are certainly sufficiently versatile to use for lots of purposes. I'm finding the Dammit Doll, p.17 helpful in these unsettled political times... or with teenagers in the house.

Dammit Doll

Face pattern...use embroidery or a permanent marker and your imagination for the features.

Attach yarn hair securely

Dammit Doll--Body Pattern: Piece, trace, sew, turn, stuff, leave open at bottom to insert legs

Leave Open

Legs, trace on wrong side of fabric, 2 layers, right sides together. Sew inside traced lines, turn, stuff, leaving top open.

Insert top of legs into bottom of body and zig zag them together SECURELY. Grab the doll by the legs and strike against a hard surface, yelling, "Dammit! Dammit! Dammit!!!

Leave Open

Author's note: Please do NOT use this doll to strike your child...or any elected official, no matter how much they provoke you.

Double Doll

The origin of Topsy Turvey dolls is shaded in mystery. When I was young in the Fifties, one end was white and the other dark--two characters joined at the waist, with a double-sided skirt that could hide one end or the other. Some suggest that these slave/mistress dolls were invented to socialize black girls into their future career of taking care of white children: Topsy and Eva in Uncle Tom's Cabin.

Story-telling flip dolls: Little Red Riding Hood and Wolf, Goldilocks and Three bears.

Today use this pattern to express two different sides of your personality or emotions: happy/sad, angry/smiling.

Wild/Sweet

Double Doll

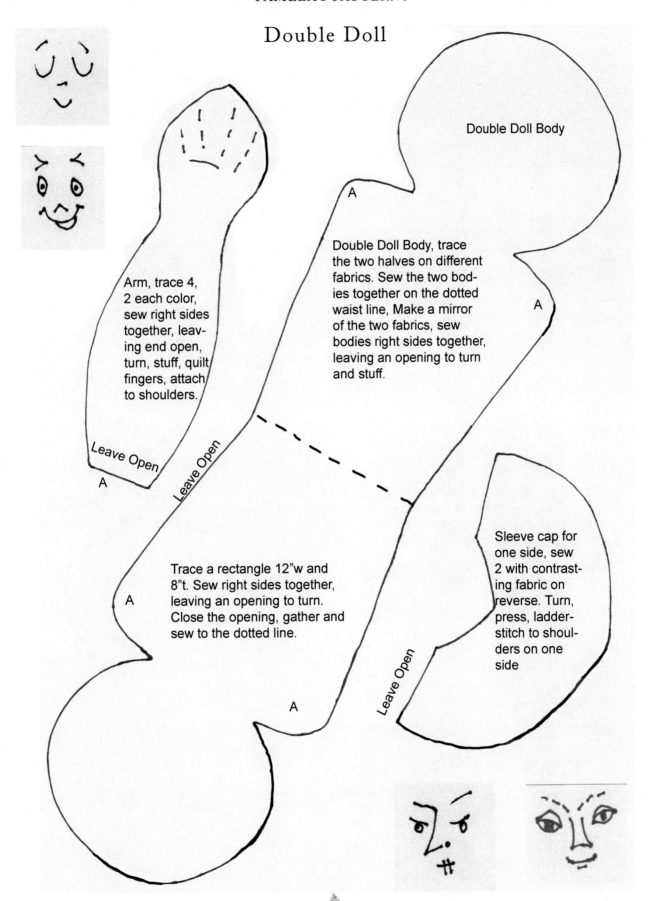

Double Doll Body

A

Double Doll Body, trace the two halves on different fabrics. Sew the two bodies together on the dotted waist line, Make a mirror of the two fabrics, sew bodies right sides together, leaving an opening to turn and stuff.

A

Arm, trace 4, 2 each color, sew right sides together, leaving end open, turn, stuff, quilt fingers, attach to shoulders.

Leave Open

Leave Open

A

Trace a rectangle 12"w and 8"t. Sew right sides together, leaving an opening to turn. Close the opening, gather and sew to the dotted line.

A

Sleeve cap for one side, sew 2 with contrasting fabric on reverse. Turn, press, ladder-stitch to shoulders on one side

Leave Open

A

Love Yourself

ARMS
CUT 4

LOVE
YOURSELF
Leave Open!

Leave Open!
CUT 2

Mount this Love Yourself
on a dowel and stick it
into a heavy base...or
even a cake!

Love Yourself

LOVE
YOURSELF

BODY
CUT 2
SEW.
TURN.
STUFF

Leave open

Leave open
for dowel

SELF PORTRAIT
BUST

Your face or famous
person's here

Cut 2
Trace, sew, clip curves
Leave bottom open A to B
With right sides together,
Sew to base, leaving a wide
opening at the back
Insert stiff cardboard and
weight, slip stitch closed

A   Leave open   © Pamela 2012   B

Leave Open

Cut a piece of stiff
cardboard a little
smaller — add that
and a weight (big
washer or stone)
inside

A   B

I did the first version of Love Yourself for Kathy Charlton, a local wine maker and community activist. She was working with our hospital to sponsor heart health awareness for women.

We are often so busy taking care of others that we don't pay enough attention to our own physical and mental health. These dolls are reminders to put ourselves first, so we have the energy to care for others and so our daughters receive a good role model for self-care.

Story Girl

It's an interesting challenge to look at our lives through making self portrait dolls (page 10). Here's a more three-dimensional approach.

The face photo is me at 4 years old and my aspirations written on the skirt with indelible marker. Mount the doll on a weighted bottle.

Self Portrait

Self Portrait at a time of Crisis: Above a doll I made in a Barb Kobe class when I was at a crisis point in a relationship, and ended up leaving the person. The body is muslin, outside zig-zag seam, stuffed and collaged with tissue paper and a photo of my face, yarn hair...very rough, but a way to think about what I was feeling.

Story Girl

Quilt between the fingers and fold hands around the wire circle of stars. Bring the arms out of the horizontal plane by folding them forward and securing with a ladder stitch. (page 75)

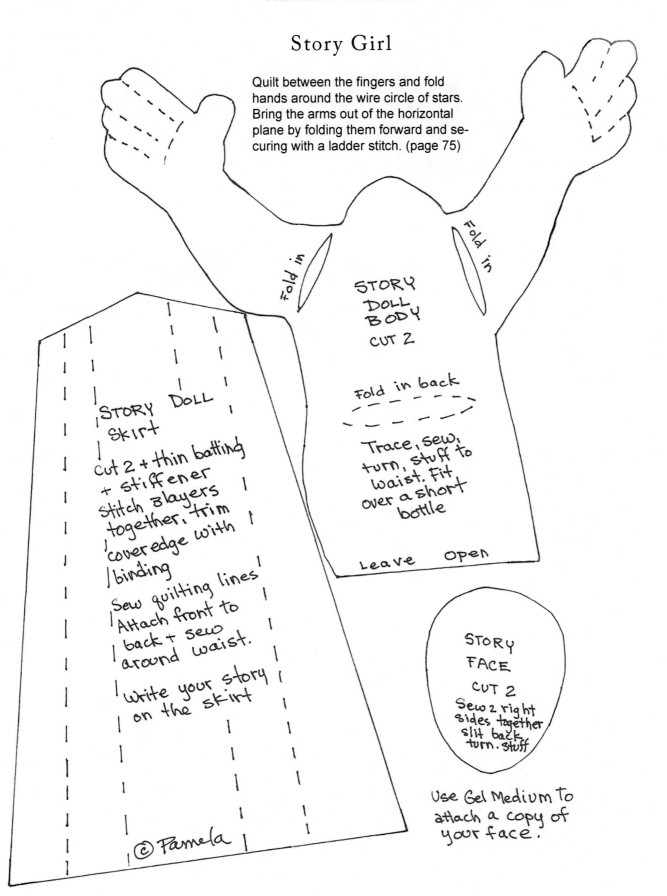

Fold in

Fold in

STORY DOLL BODY CUT 2

Fold in back

Trace, sew, turn, stuff to waist. Fit over a short bottle

Leave Open

STORY DOLL Skirt

Cut 2 + thin batting + stiffener Stitch 3 layers together, trim cover edge with binding

Sew quilting lines Attach front to back + sew around waist.

Write your story on the skirt

© Pamela

STORY FACE CUT 2 Sew 2 right sides together slit back turn. stuff

Use Gel Medium to attach a copy of your face.

Fish/Bird Woman

Imp 2

Fish Woman: The face is the only gusset, Dimension is achieved through multiple 2-piece parts.

Imp2: I love making and decorating endless numbers of these little icons... then I always have something to give away. I keep a box of scraps by my sewing machine so I can piece up some sheets big enough to make dolls.

The face is pewter from Art Girlz, different-sized beads, piecing, quilting, and decorative stitches up the body, which is quilted into 3 parallel sections with beads at the bottom.

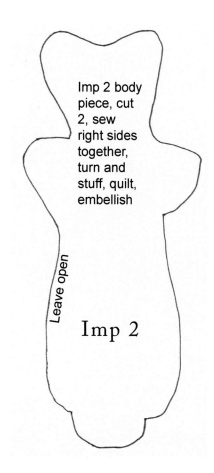

Imp 2 body piece, cut 2, sew right sides together, turn and stuff, quilt, embellish

Leave open

Imp 2

Fish Woman Pattern

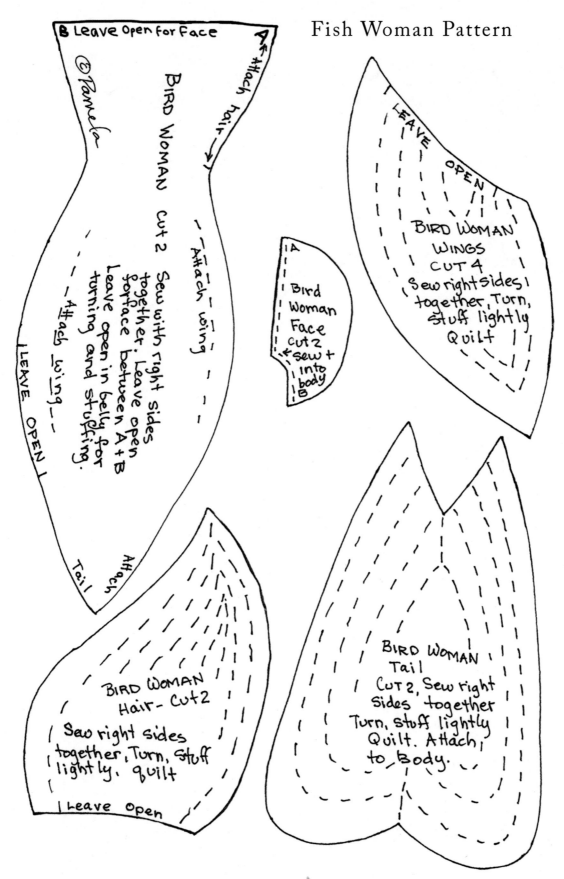

B Leave Open for Face

A ← Attach hair →

@Pamela

BIRD WOMAN Cut 2 Sew with right sides together. Leave open for face. Leave open in belly for turning and stuffing.

-- Attach wing

-- Attach wing --

LEAVE OPEN

Attach Tail

A
Bird Woman Face cut 2 ← Sew + into body
B

LEAVE OPEN

BIRD WOMAN WINGS CUT 4 Sew right sides together, Turn, stuff lightly Quilt

BIRD WOMAN Hair - cut 2 Sew right sides together, Turn, Stuff lightly, quilt

Leave Open

BIRD WOMAN Tail cut 2, Sew right sides together Turn, stuff lightly Quilt. Attach to Body.

Embrace Life With Joy

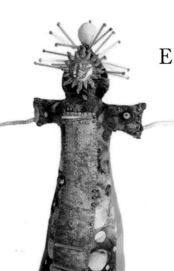

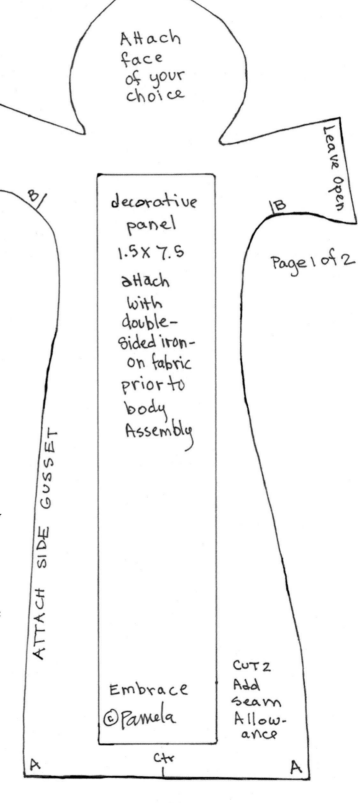

Attach face of your choice

Leave Open

Leave Open

B

B

ATTACH SIDE GUSSET

decorative panel 1.5 x 7.5 attach with double-sided iron-on fabric prior to body Assembly

Page 1 of 2

Embrace ©Pamela

CUT 2 Add Seam Allow-ance

A

Ctr

A

A perfect doll with which to express your intentions...I used a bright and joyful combination of yellows, contrasting purple, and turquoise for the gussets, backing the Dupioni silk with iron-on interfacing. Make a decorative panel with beading, embroidery, or special fabric and use double-sided iron-on interfacing to attach it to the front of the doll before assembling the body.

Sew the side gussets to the front with the right sides together, then sew the back to the front, leaving the bottom open.

Cut a 1.75" x 14" strip of something pretty and sew around the bottom of the body with right sides together.

Add iron-on interfacing to the base and add to the body, right sides together, leaving enough of an opening to insert the cardboard base.

Turn right side out and add stones or heavy washers to the inside bottom of the doll after stuffing the top. I inserted a weathered stick through the arms before stuffing, but then you have to stuff around the stick, so make the arms longer and use something different for hands or no hands.

Embrace Life With Joy

I used a beading needle and special beading thread to sew through long yellow beads and attach them with a seed bead, going back through the long bead and into the head.

A sun charm for the face. A larger bead on top of the head, more beads on the body...let your imagination run wild!

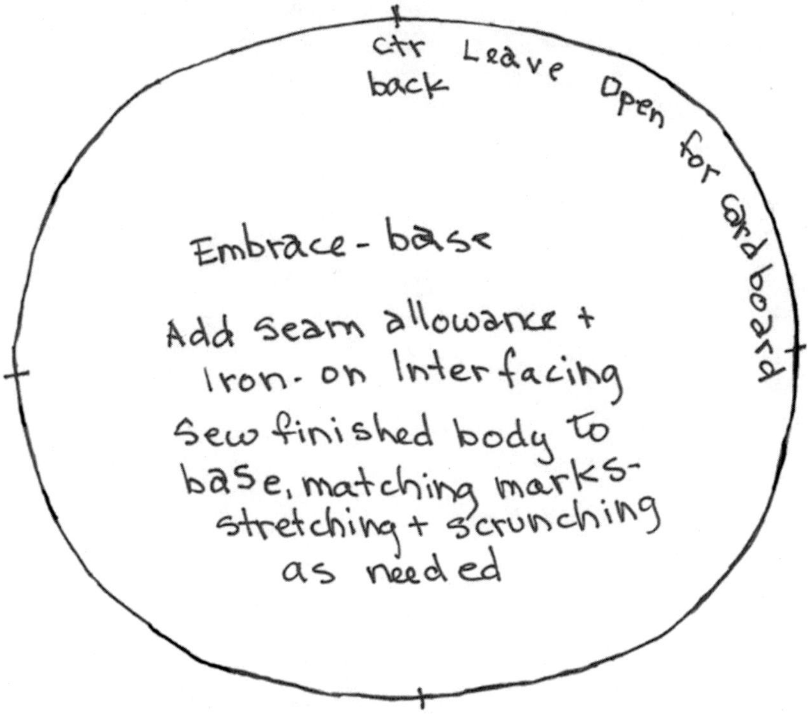

ctr back Leave Open for cardboard

Embrace - base

Add Seam allowance + Iron- on Interfacing

Sew finished body to base, matching marks-stretching + scrunching as needed

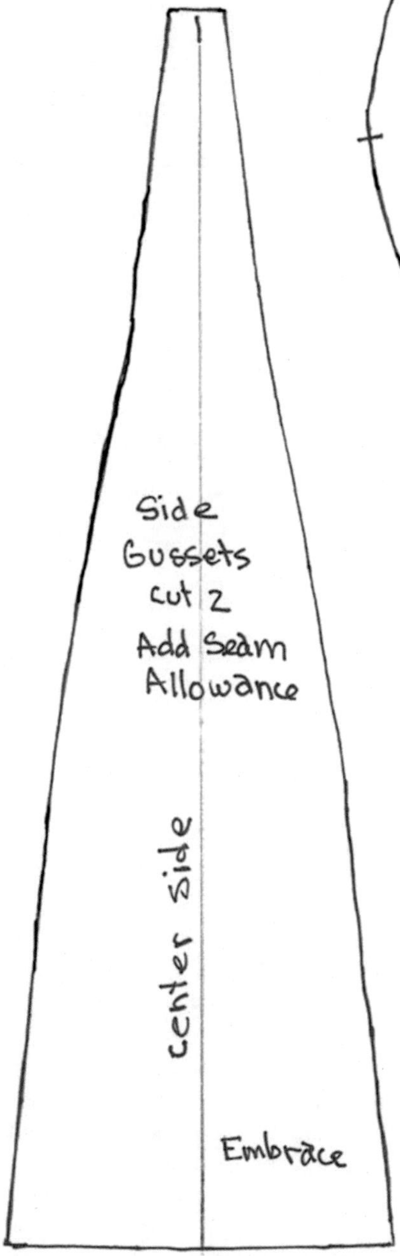

Side Gussets cut 2 Add Seam Allowance

center side

Embrace

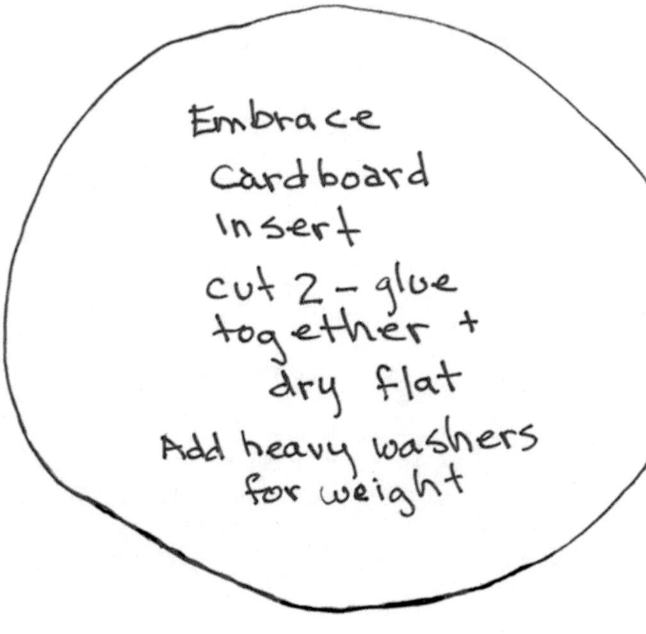

Embrace Cardboard Insert cut 2 - glue together + dry flat Add heavy washers for weight

White Angels, (page 5): Sew strips of white-on-white fabric together, using a short stitch. Trace Body fronts on the back of the sewn strips, cut out, leaving seam allowance. Print high-contrast faces (like the ones on page 19) on a sheet of white muslin, leaving space to zig-zag each face onto an angel front. Then sew body fronts to plain white fabric, sewing on your traced line, right sides together, turn and stuff, close opening with a ladder stitch. Add charm hands, bead or charm feet.

Sew, turn, stuff, close pairs of wings and machine quilt. Add beads and hearts and fluffy white angel hair with hanging loop.

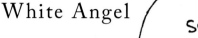

White Angel

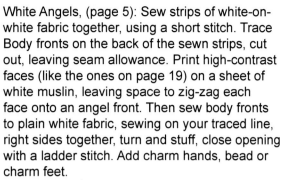

Sew on a Face

ANGEL

PIECE 2
TRACE, SEW,
CUT, TURN, STUFF

Sew on charm hands + feet

Leave Open

ANGEL WINGS 2 Layers, Trace, Sew, cut, turn, stuff

Leave Open

Christmas Angel 2012

I bought a collection of hand-dyed cottons on a trip to the Shakespeare Festival in Ashland, Oregon, with my brother, Hugh, and his wife, Connie. Rather than keep this treasure trove folded up and put away, I designed my 2012 angel to use as many different small pieces as possible.

I cut, sewed, and stuffed a basket full at a time, so I could experiment with different fabric combinations. I Love having hand work to do while watching movies on my studio laptop, so I made a bunch of these beauties...I think it was my most popular Annual Angel design. I got to use the best fabrics...and still have some left over.

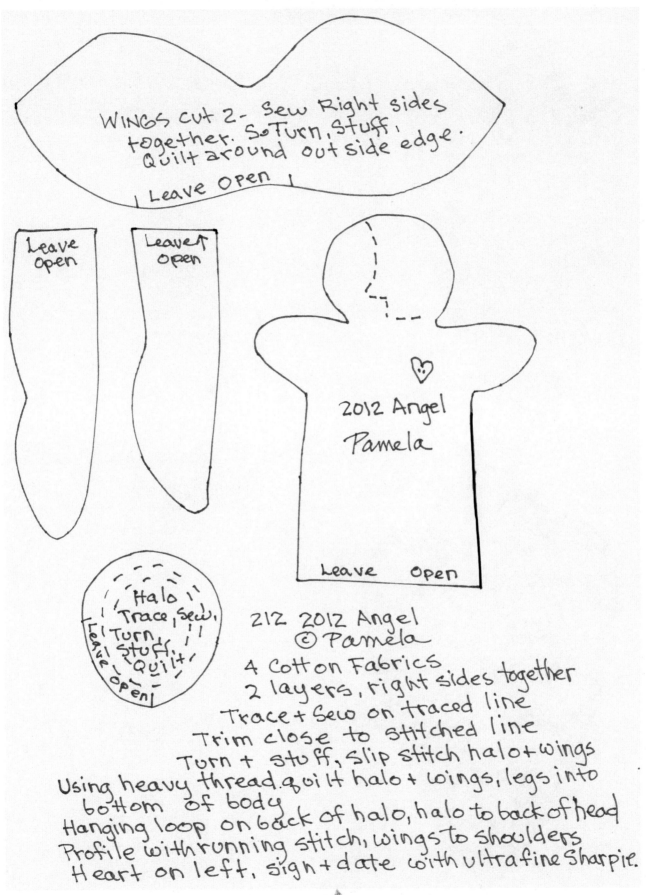

WINGS cut 2 - Sew Right sides together. SoTurn, Stuff, Quilt around out side edge.
Leave Open

Leave open

Leave open

2012 Angel
Pamela

Leave Open

Halo
Trace, Sew,
Turn,
Stuff,
Quilt
Leave open

212 2012 Angel
© Pamela
4 Cotton Fabrics
2 layers, right sides together
Trace + Sew on traced line
Trim close to stitched line
Turn + stuff, Slip stitch halo + wings
Using heavy thread, quilt halo + wings, legs into bottom of body
Hanging loop on back of halo, halo to back of head
Profile with running stitch, wings to shoulders
Heart on left, sign + date with ultra fine Sharpie.

Blessing Doll

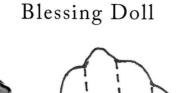

When I turned Transformative Doll Making into an online class, I did patterns that could be created in fabric or cloth, like this Blessing Doll. Try more patterns both ways!

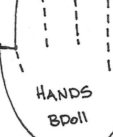

HANDS

BDoll

For Paper Cut 2
Cut Door in top layer

DOOR for	PAPER DOLL
FOLD	FOLD

BLESSING DOLL

BODY

Cut 2

For fabric
Sew on traced
lines – leave
an opening
to turn &
stuff

Pamela

Blessing Doll

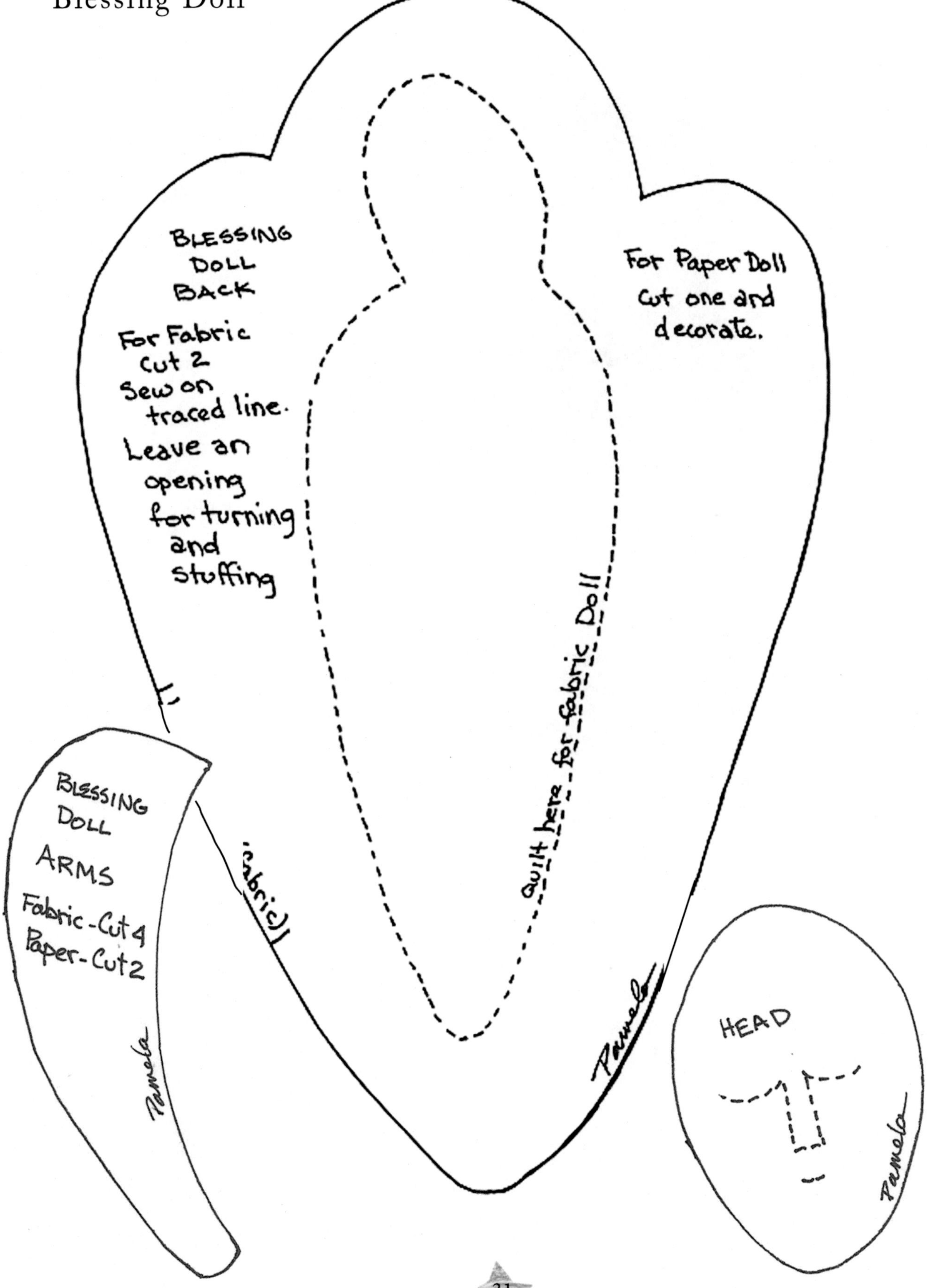

BLESSING
DOLL
BACK

For Fabric
Cut 2
Sew on
traced line.

Leave an
opening
for turning
and
stuffing

For Paper Doll
Cut one and
decorate.

Quilt here for fabric Doll

'abric)

BLESSING
DOLL

ARMS

Fabric - Cut 4
Paper - Cut 2

Pamela

Pamela

HEAD

Pamela

31

Sisters

Sew the front and back body with right sides together, leaving the bottom open. Sew the gusset to the bottom of the body, leaving the back open.

Turn the body, start stitching the heads, as you stuff the bottom, insert a piece of stiff cardboard, with a fishing weight or stone wrapped in stuffing just above the base to help the piece stand securely.

Use a ladder stitch to close the back opening.

Make 2 or 4 arms, sew right sides together, turn, and stuff. Attach to the shoulders with a ladder stitch or a button.

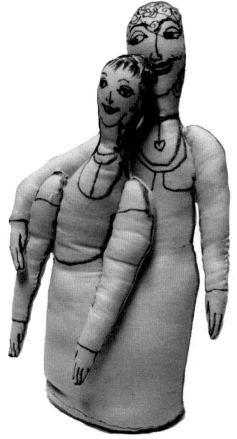

This pattern expresses a relationship between two sisters or two friends. You may use copies of old or current photos printed on silk, cotton, or paper. You can see how differently the same pattern can be expressed in Erica Cleveland's muslin with indelible marker interpretation to the right. She added extra arms to make the pose more loving. Leaving just a small space between the figures makes them overlap.

I pieced my version of the body using short stitches for the piecing, then traced the pattern reversed on the back side of the front piece. You may embellish with lace, buttons, embroidery, beads...or anything else you have on hand.

Sisters Pattern

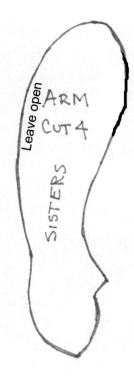

Leave open
ARM
CUT 4

SISTERS

Use iron-on interfacing on the inside of the fabric base to help keep it flat.
Add a piece of stiff cardboard cut smaller than the base and a fishing weight or stone to help with standing.

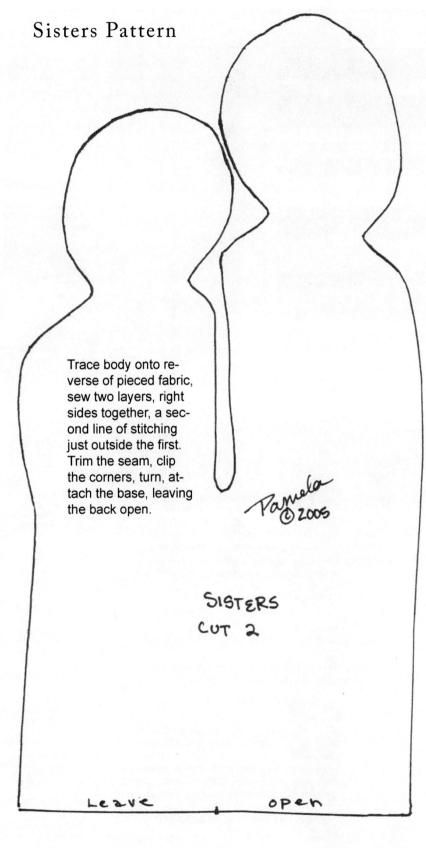

Trace body onto reverse of pieced fabric, sew two layers, right sides together, a second line of stitching just outside the first. Trim the seam, clip the corners, turn, attach the base, leaving the back open.

Pamela © 2005

SISTERS
CUT 2

SISTERS
Base
CUT 1 WITH SEAM ALL
Cut 1 from card board-
may need to trim
card board

Leave   open

Blue-Faced Angel

The hanging point is just below where the wings are attached. To test: put a straight pin where you think the hanging loop should be attached. Wind a thread around the pin and test her balance.

Box Doll

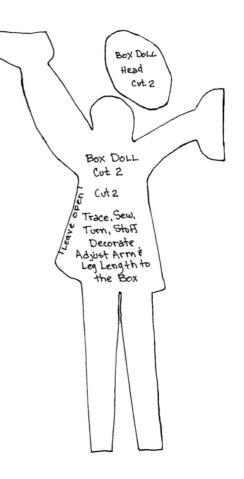

I created this small doll pattern to fit inside an antique box. To make one to fit your box, measure the box opening, copy the pattern, and scan it, then enlarge the pattern to fit the measurements of your box.

I did just a little bit of needle modeling on the face: pinched the nose, eyebrows, small mouth, to make it a bit more realistic.

I used beads for embellishment, make your decoration fit your theme.

BOX DOLL
Head
Cut 2

BOX DOLL
Cut 2

Cut 2

Leave open

Trace, Sew,
Turn, Stuff
Decorate,
Adjust Arm &
Leg Length to
the Box

Blue-Faced Angel

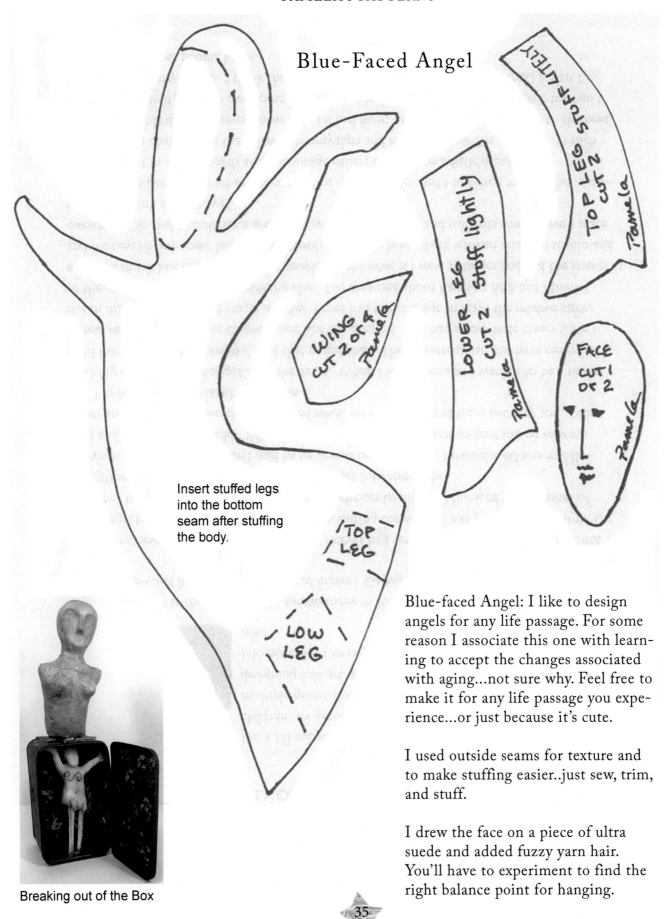

TOP LEG STUFF FLATELY
CUT 2
Pamela

WING
CUT 2 OR 4
Pamela

LOWER LEG
CUT 2 Stuff lightly
Pamela

FACE
CUT 1
OF 2
Pamela

Insert stuffed legs into the bottom seam after stuffing the body.

/TOP
/LEG

/ LOW \
\ LEG /

Breaking out of the Box

Blue-faced Angel: I like to design angels for any life passage. For some reason I associate this one with learning to accept the changes associated with aging...not sure why. Feel free to make it for any life passage you experience...or just because it's cute.

I used outside seams for texture and to make stuffing easier..just sew, trim, and stuff.

I drew the face on a piece of ultra suede and added fuzzy yarn hair. You'll have to experiment to find the right balance point for hanging.

Message Woman

Message
WOMAN
FACE

Quilt Nose, eye
eyebrows

Leave Open

CUT 2
Trace
Sew
Turn
Stuff

Leave Open

MESSAGE

Boot
trace
sew
right
sides
turn
Stuff

Leave open

MESSAGE
Arms
cut 4
Sew
Turn
Stuff.

Attach
to body
C with
beads

Leave Open

Message
Boot 2

Blind
Stitch
legs to
bottom
gusset.

MESSAGE WOMAN

Body- Piece + Cut 2

Sew on the traced line

Above see an older version of the Message Woman: differently-shaped body. Arms and fingers
are fabric-wrapped pipe cleaners so they can be
posed. Longer, skinnier shape.

©Pamela

B   Leave   open   A

MESSAGE WOMAN
BASE - CUT 1 + Iron-on
Interfacing
Add Seam Allowance

Leave Open

MESSAGE WOMAN ☐

Piece 10" x6" for body front and
back
Trace pattern backwards onto
the back of pieced piece
Sew front to back with right sides
together, leaving the bottom open.
Use short stitches and make a
second line of stitching just
outside the first.
Trim just outside second line
of stitching
Add iron-on interfacing to wrong
side of base
Sew base gusset to body,
leaving open in back. turn
Add stiff cardboard inside
the base, stuff.
Add hair, embellishments,
embroidered or drawn aspiration
on the back.

Friends

Friends are flat. The pattern to the right is for the two-in-one doll above, with outside seam covered with shiny binding. Faces are Fimo clay, but could be anything.
The three others are made with bright felt and embroidered faces. (photo p 74)

Enlarge these patterns and cut from felt. Outside seams.

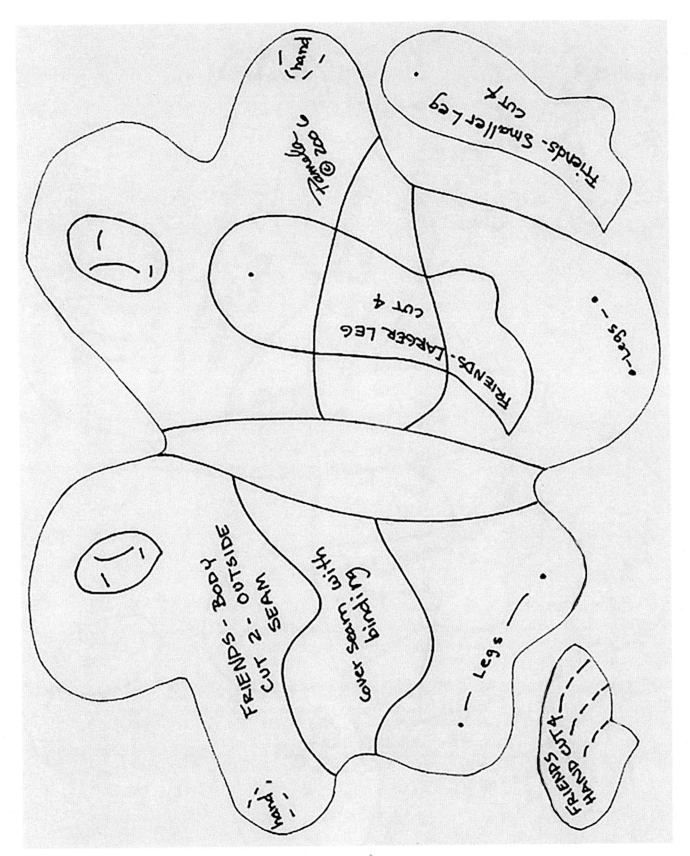

Big Fleece COMMERCIAL PATTERNS 4

I sold many, many dolls I made from these patterns, as well as the patterns themselves at craft shows and online for thirty or more years.

Two sizes and a different color scheme make a world of difference in character.

BIG FLEECE: enlarge the pattern to be as big as your child and use fleece to be nice and cuddly. Use outside seams on the head and arms, the legs are tubes. Fingers and toes are long, narrow rectangles with pipe cleaners inside, then they are sewn into the hand and foot seams. Wrap yarn around a rectangle of cardboard and sew along one edge to make nice shaggy hair.

The eyes and mouth can be buttons sewn down with a bead, button knees help the legs bend. The nose is pinched and sewn side to side, and the other features are bold.

The feet have a gusset on the bottom, Bring the top seam to the bottom gusset and insert the toes before sewing.

The body can be pieced with a bottom gusset...don't put weight into this one if it will be played with.

Big Fleece

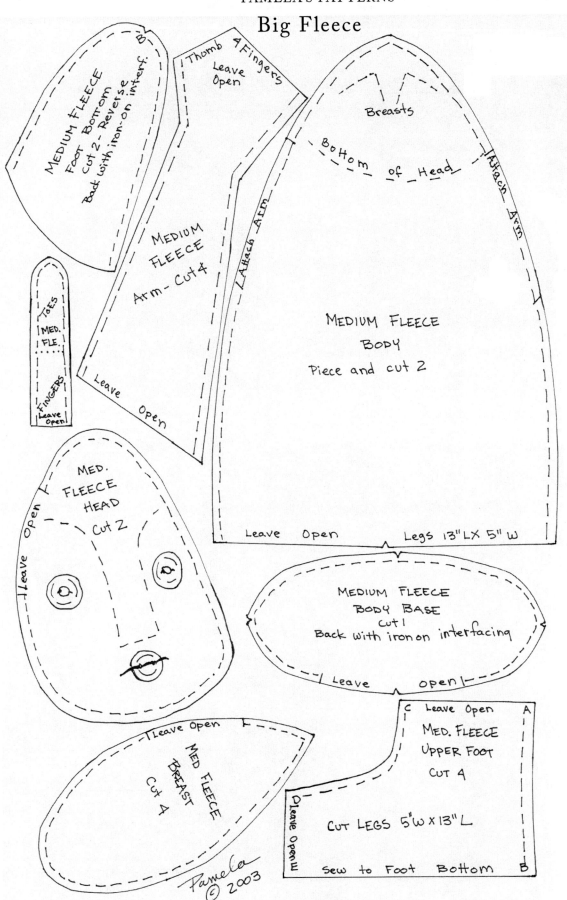

MEDIUM FLEECE
Foot Bottom
Cut 2 - Reverse
Back with iron-on interf.

Thumb 4 Fingers
Leave Open

Breasts

Bottom of Head

Attach Arm

MEDIUM FLEECE
Arm - Cut 4

Attach Arm

Leave Open

TOES
MED. FLE.
FINGERS
Leave Open

MEDIUM FLEECE
BODY
Piece and cut 2

MED. FLEECE HEAD
Cut 2

Leave Open

Leave Open   Legs 13"L X 5"W

MEDIUM FLEECE
BODY BASE
Cut 1
Back with iron on interfacing

Leave   open

Leave Open

MED FLEECE
BREAST
Cut 4

C Leave Open A
MED. FLEECE
UPPER FOOT
CUT 4

D Leave Open

CUT LEGS 5"W X 13"L

E Sew to Foot Bottom B

Pamela
© 2003

Ancestor Doll

Early
Version

Experiment with variation in faces,
on paper attached to cardboard or
printed on fabric. Scan and repro-
duce antique faces from your own
ancestors or find some online. Add
costume and appropriate decorations for the period.

Ancestor Doll
Pattern

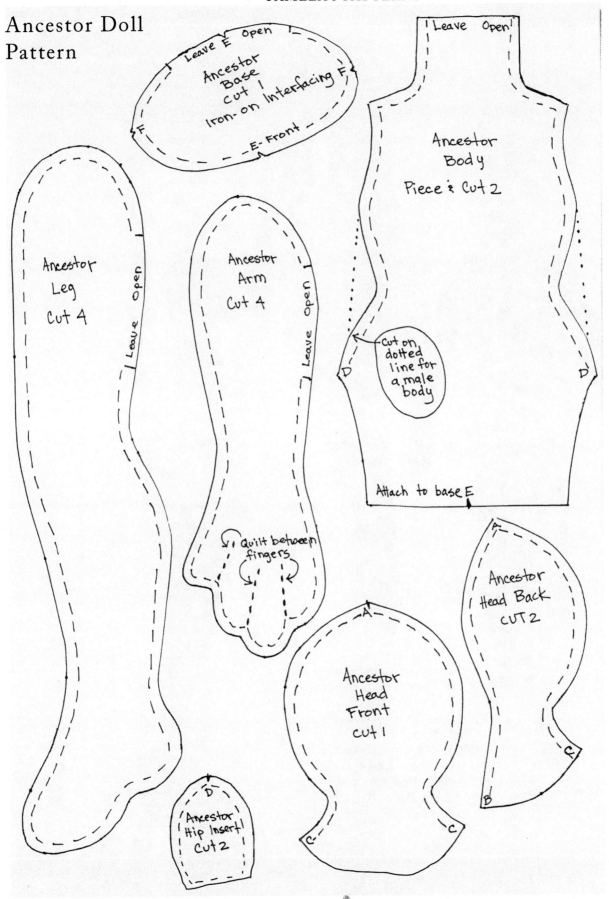

Leave E Open

Ancestor
Base
Cut 1
Iron-on Interfacing F

F

E-Front

Leave Open

Ancestor
Body
Piece & Cut 2

Cut on dotted line for a male body

D

D

Attach to base E

Ancestor
Leg
Cut 4

Leave Open

Ancestor
Arm
Cut 4

Leave Open

Quilt between fingers

A

Ancestor
Head Back
CUT 2

C

A

Ancestor
Head
Front
cut 1

B

C

D

Ancestor
Hip Insert
Cut 2

C

Button Face

Button Face
Head
cut 2

cut a 1" slit
center front
for turning

Button Face: simple starter project
Sew the shoulders to the body, front
and back. Press and sew front and back
bodies with right sides together. Stiffen
the base and sew to the body, right sides
together, turn, and stuff.
Sew the two heads all around the outside
edge, cut a slit in the front, turn and stuff.
Use the smaller circle, turned to cover the
hole in the head. Sew on a button as the
face. Bead "feelers" on top of the head.
Sew, turn, stuff arms, legs, wings. Buttons
attach arms, ladder stitch to attach head
and legs and wings

Button Face Pattern

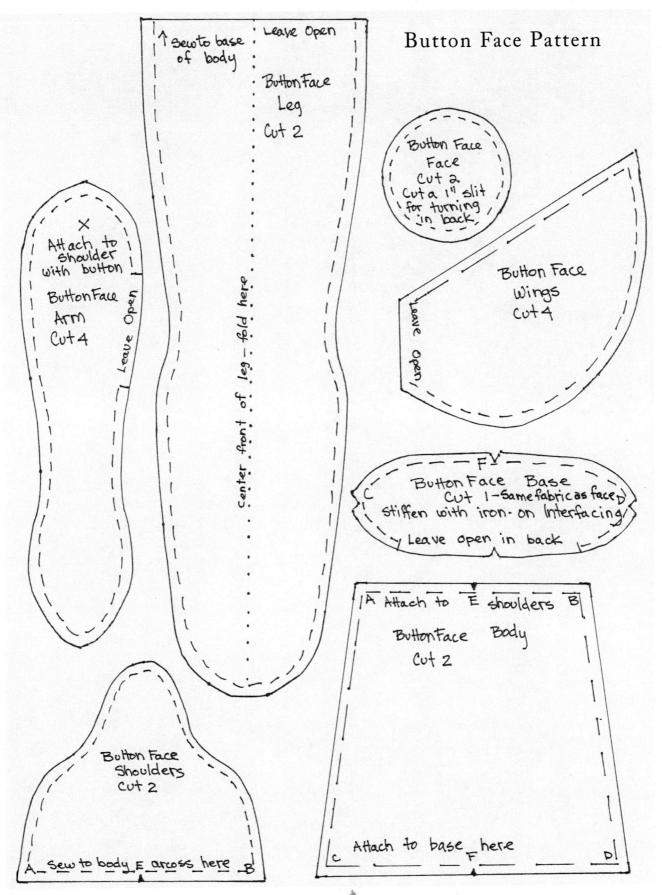

↑ Sew to base of body

Leave Open

Button Face
Leg
Cut 2

center front of leg – fold here

Button Face
Face
Cut 2
Cut a 1" slit
for turning
in back.

Button Face
Wings
Cut 4

Leave Open

X
Attach to
shoulder
with button

Button Face
Arm
Cut 4

Leave Open

F
C Button Face Base D
Cut 1 – Same fabric as face
Stiffen with iron-on Interfacing
Leave open in back

A Attach to E shoulders B

Button Face Body
Cut 2

Attach to base here
C F D

Button Face
Shoulders
Cut 2

A Sew to body E across here B

Cuties

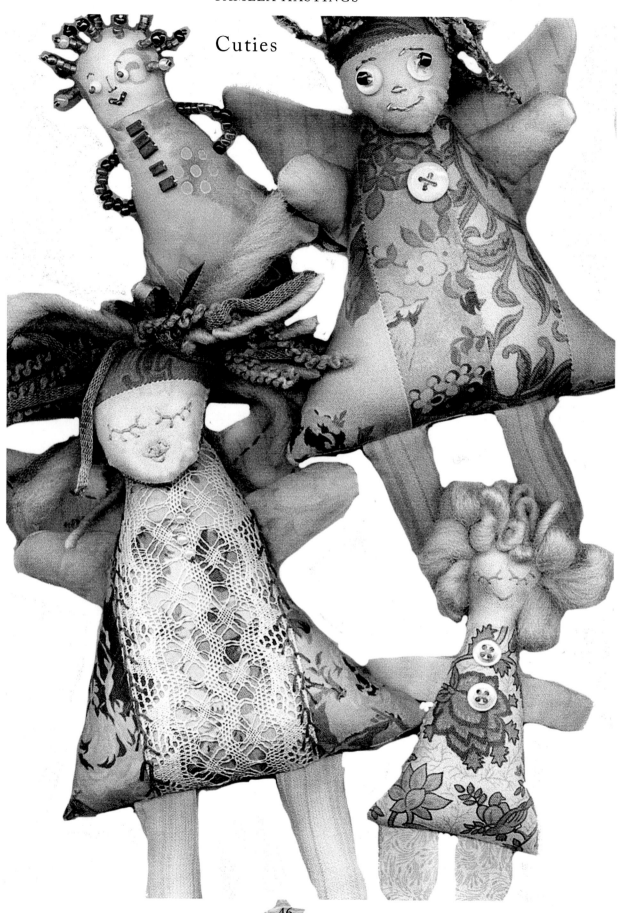

Cuties Pattern

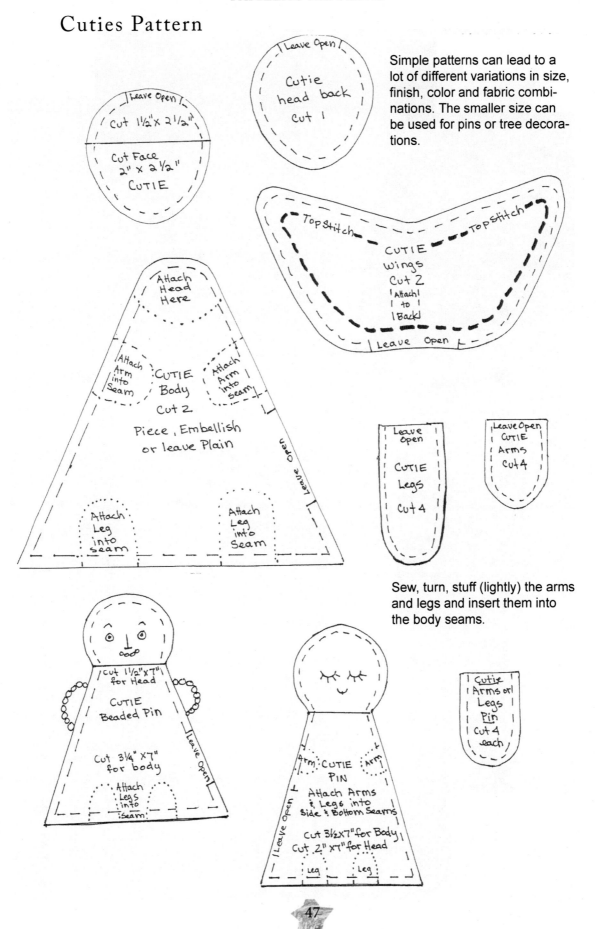

Leave Open

Cut 1½" x 2½"

Cut Face
2" x 2½"
CUTIE

Leave Open

Cutie
head back
Cut 1

Simple patterns can lead to a lot of different variations in size, finish, color and fabric combinations. The smaller size can be used for pins or tree decorations.

Top Stitch   Top Stitch

CUTIE
Wings
Cut 2
Attach
to
Back

Leave Open

Attach
Head
Here

Attach
Arm
into
Seam

CUTIE
Body
Cut 2

Attach
Arm
into
Seam

Piece, Embellish
or leave Plain

Leave Open

Attach
Leg
into
seam

Attach
Leg
into
Seam

Leave
open

CUTIE
Legs
Cut 4

Leave Open
CUTIE
Arms
Cut 4

Sew, turn, stuff (lightly) the arms and legs and insert them into the body seams.

Cut 1½" x 7"
for Head

CUTIE
Beaded Pin

Cut 3¼" x 7"
for body

Leave Open

Attach
Legs
into
Seam

Arm CUTIE Arm
PIN

Attach Arms
& Legs into
Side & Bottom Seams

Cut 3½x7" for Body
Cut 2" x7" for Head

Leg   Leg

Leave Open

Cutie
Arms or
Legs
Pin
Cut 4
each

Damsel

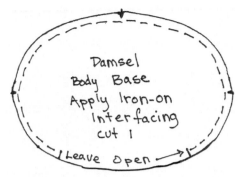

Damsel
Body Base
Apply Iron-on
Interfacing
cut 1
← Leave Open →

Damsel...a more feminine approach to doll making, with a crown of beads or beads and ribbons and as much other embellishment as you desire. I like piecing, which allows for a lot of different color/pattern combinations. Don't forget the gusset at the bottom of the body.

Muslin for the head, sewn all the way around for a smooth circle. Cut a slit for turning and hanging, cover that with the headdress. Use light indelible markers for the facial features and a little needle modeling to pinch out a nose and quilt under eyebrows. Small red beads in the corners of the eyes for a more lifelike effect.

Sew a hanging loop on the back of the headdress. Button breasts...great way to play with different fabric combinations.

As you can see, I've used the same basic approach: body with gusset, separate arms and legs, to create a variety of different looks...do your own experimenting

Damsel Pattern

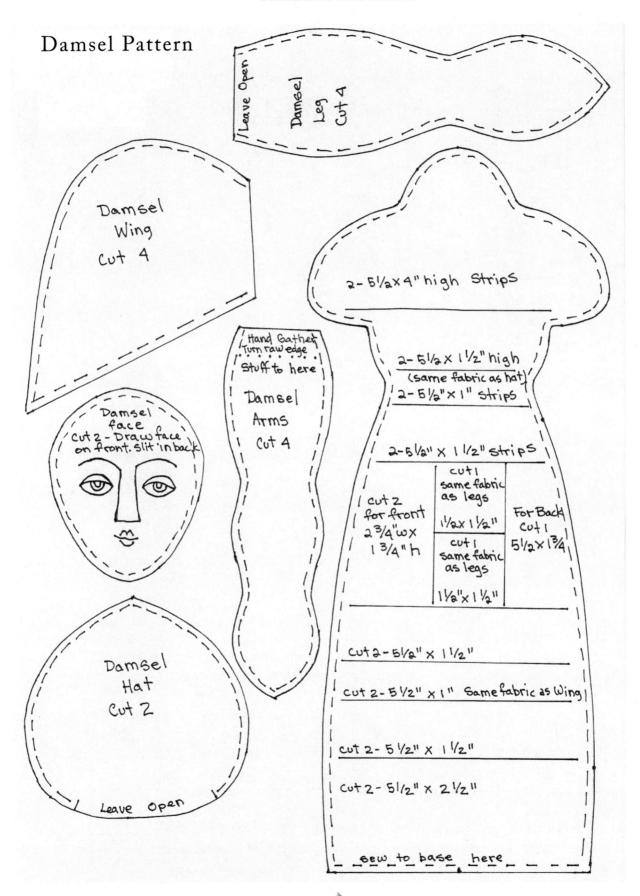

Leave Open

Damsel
Leg
Cut 4

Damsel
Wing
Cut 4

Hand Gather
Turn raw edge
Stuff to here

Damsel
Arms
Cut 4

Damsel
face
Cut 2 - Draw face
on front. slit in back

2 - 5½ x 4" high Strips

2 - 5½ x 1½" high
(same fabric as hat)
2 - 5½" x 1" Strips

2 - 5½" x 1½" Strips

cut 1
same fabric
as legs

1½ x 1½"

cut 1
same fabric
as legs

1½" x 1½"

cut 2
for front
2¾"w x
1¾"h

For Back
Cut 1
5½ x 1¾

Damsel
Hat
Cut 2

Leave Open

Cut 2 - 5½" x 1½"

Cut 2 - 5½" x 1" Same fabric as Wing

Cut 2 - 5½" x 1½"

Cut 2 - 5½" x 2½"

sew to base here

Wild Women

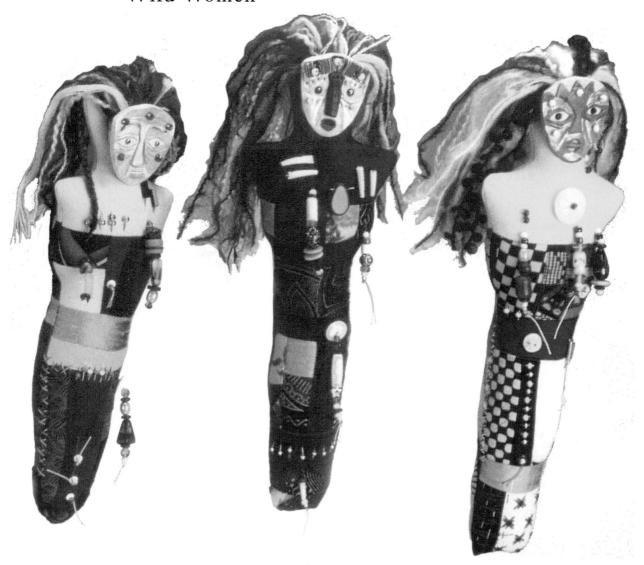

Wild Woman was one of the first commercial patterns I designed. I was having fun making body parts from Fimo clay and had a Goodwill toaster oven totally dedicated to clay baking, out in the garage. It was fun to roll out, cut, and decorate tons of faces, like these and the ones on Friends, page 38. Every time I learned a new technique, I could design a doll to showcase it...You can, too!

I pieced the bodies, using a short sewing machine stitch, then traced the body shape on the back of the pieced piece. I had a lot of ultra suede around from previous purchases, so made the top of ultra suede, but you can use any firmly-woven fabric...or back the fabric with shirt-weight iron-on interfacing. Sew the upper body to the lower body, then the front and back together with two lines of stitching and an opening at the side to turn and stuff.

Use a combination of yarns wrapped around cardboard, stitched together at one and cut at the other side for hair. Sew that to the front of the head, then use sturdy thread to attach the face on top, using beads to hold the face down. Add plenty of tribal embellishments and attach a hanging loop to the back.

Wild Woman Pattern

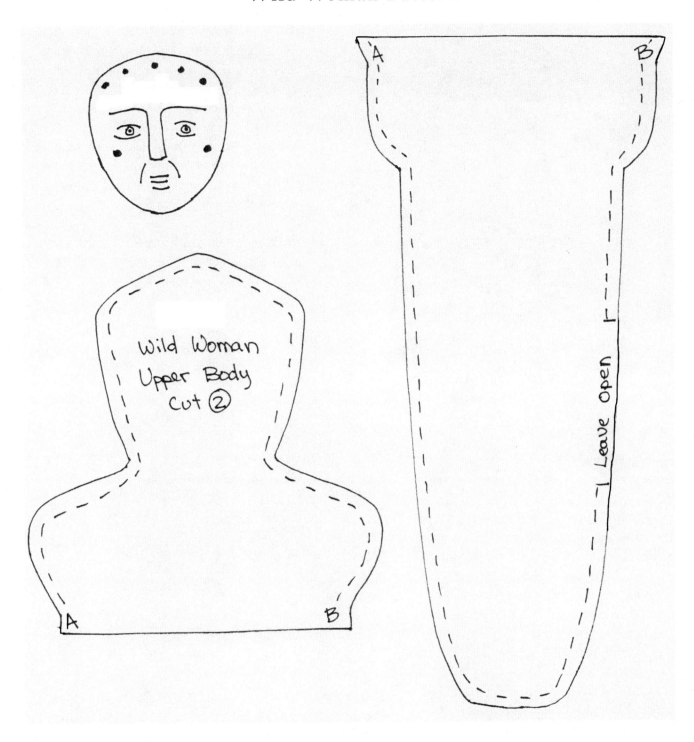

Look at African sculptures for inspiration for additional shapes. Make the body longer or shorter, experiment with different materials for faces...Crayola Model Magic is a paper clay that can be shaped easily, air-dries firmly, painted with acrylic paints, and stitched through to attach it. You could also use stiff cardboard with a face collaged or drawn on. Use a string of beads or a fabric shape to make arms to sew to the body. You may experiment with the arms from another doll in this book, then design your own.

Wise Woman

The Wise Woman is another early and simple pattern. The head has a two-part front and a top gusset, but the other body parts are just two pieces each. Enlarge the size of the pattern as much as you like.

Make the head from unbleached muslin and use acrylic paints, following the face template. I love the pointy teeth, but you need not put those onto your doll.

You could make the body from muslin instead of piecing, and just paint or collage it.

I used my big supply of ultra suede for the arms and legs, but you can use any tightly-woven fabric, sewing with right sides together, then turning and stuffing. Or back a stretchy fabric with shirt-weight iron-on interfacing. Quilt to separate fingers. Change the shape of the hands, feet, and body as you will.

Attach the arms and legs with buttons so they can be posed. use stitching and sequins to embellish.

The wig is the varied yarns wrapped around a cardboard, sewn at one edge and cut at the other. Don't be too careful attaching the wig to the head...A messy look adds to the overall image.

Wise Woman Pattern

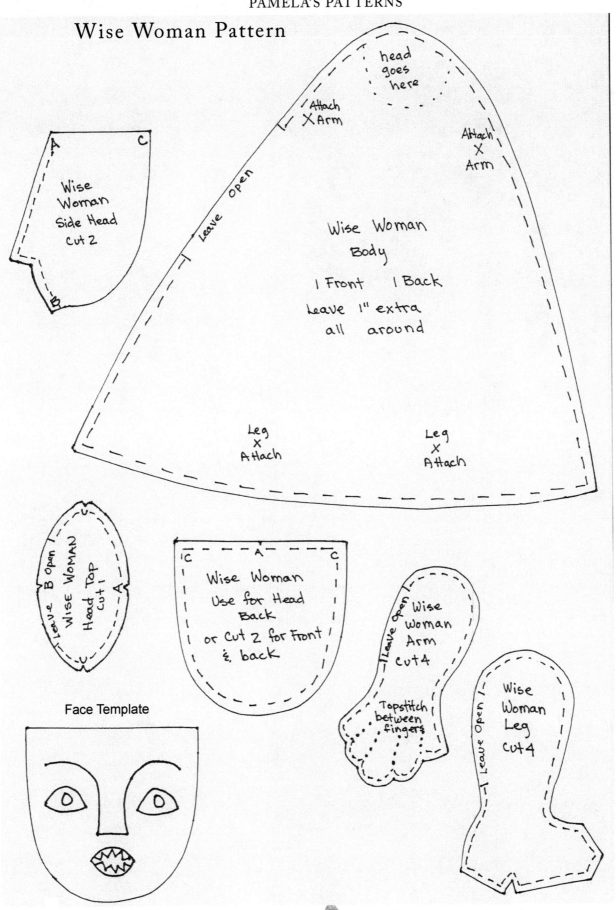

Wise Woman Side Head Cut 2

A   C

B

Attach X Arm

head goes here

Attach X Arm

Leave Open

Wise Woman Body

1 Front   1 Back

Leave 1" extra all around

Leg X Attach

Leg X Attach

Leave B Open   Wise Woman Head Top Cut 1

C   A   C

Wise Woman Use for Head Back or Cut 2 for Front & back

Leave Open   Wise Woman Arm Cut 4

Topstitch between fingers

Leave Open   Wise Woman Leg Cut 4

Face Template

53

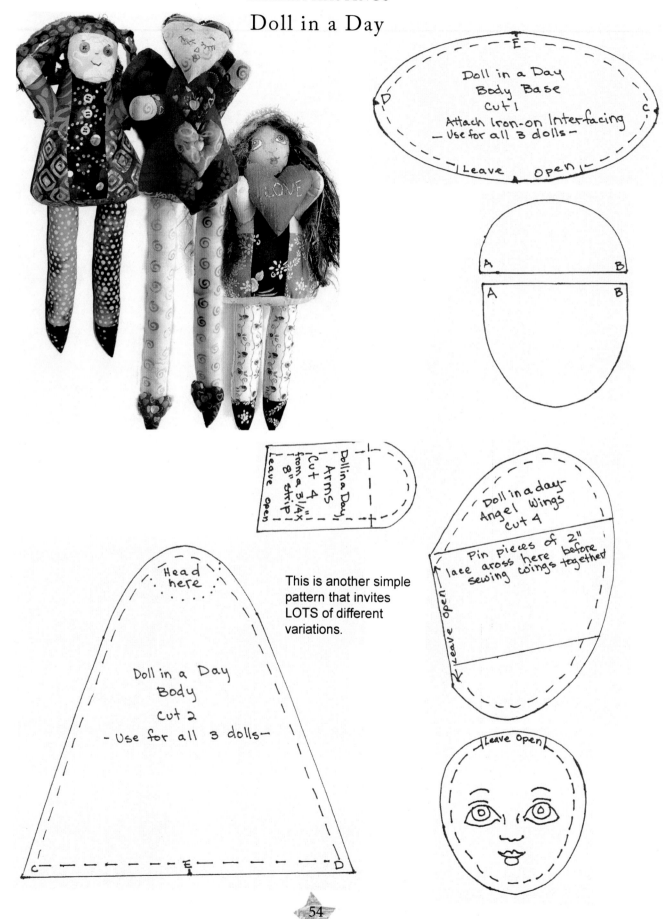

PAMELA HASTINGS
Doll in a Day

Doll in a Day
Body Base
Cut 1
Attach Iron-on Interfacing
— Use for all 3 dolls —

Leave Open

E

D

C

A   B

A   B

Doll in a Day
Arms
Cut 4
from a 3/4 x
8" strip

Leave Open

Doll in a day—
Angel Wings
Cut 4

Pin pieces of 2"
lace across here before
sewing wings together

Leave open

Head here

Doll in a Day
Body
Cut 2
— Use for all 3 dolls —

This is another simple
pattern that invites
LOTS of different
variations.

C   E   D

Leave Open

54

Doll in a Day Pattern

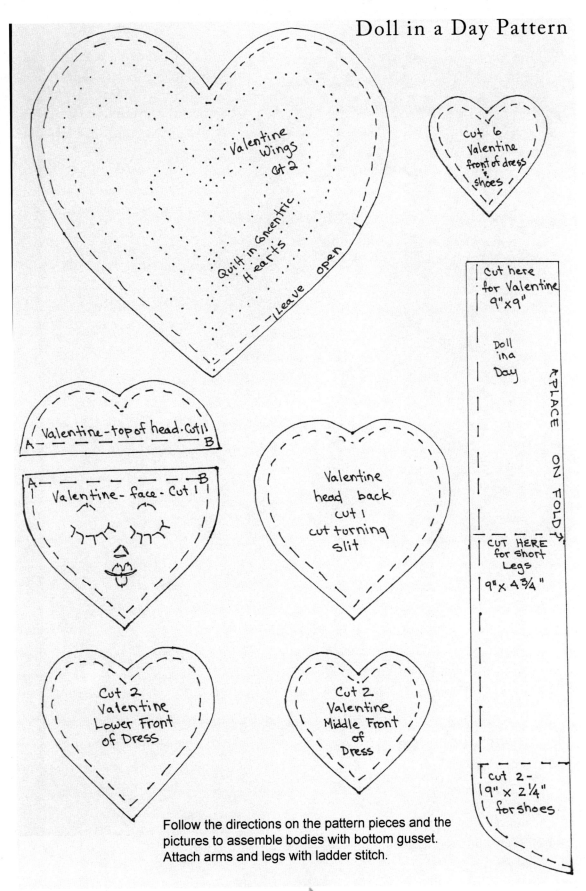

Valentine
Wings
Cut 2

Quilt in Concentric
Hearts

Leave open

Cut 6
Valentine
front of dress
& shoes

Valentine - top of head · Cut 1
A B

A B
Valentine - face - Cut 1

Valentine
head back
cut 1
cut turning
slit

Cut here
for Valentine
9" x 9"

Doll
in a
Day

PLACE ON FOLD

CUT HERE
for short
Legs
9" x 4¾"

Cut 2
Valentine
Lower Front
of Dress

Cut 2
Valentine
Middle Front
of
Dress

Cut 2 -
9" x 2¼"
for shoes

Follow the directions on the pattern pieces and the
pictures to assemble bodies with bottom gusset.
Attach arms and legs with ladder stitch.

Hot Flash

I designed the first Hot Flash doll (left) in the eighties, the second was the topic of an article in Quilting Arts Magazine. The subject is universal, so I did a book and an online class entitled Hot Flash, A Celebration.

Women took this concept as a rite of passage, a way of celebrating big changes in their forties and beyond. It certainly seems like a phenomena to be celebrated with vibrant colors and embellishment.

For the Hot Flash Doll to the left, please enlarge the pattern pieces to fit on 11" x 14" paper at a copy shop.

For the larger Hot Flash, pick a selection of bright and shiny fabrics, using Iron-on interfacing to stabilize any stretchy pieces. Cut out all the pattern pieces, doing the head in unbleached muslin, so you can paint the features with acrylic paints. Piece the remaining body parts with your bright fabrics, then trace the pattern pieces on the back with an extra-fine sharpie. Seam allowance is included in the pattern piece.

If you prefer, you can make the whole doll from muslin and paint the entire body, or use a bright fabric for the whole body, rather than piecing.

Hot Flash 2 Pattern

Use Hot Flash 2 for a warm up project. Print your face on paper or cloth to celebrate your Power Surge of Life.

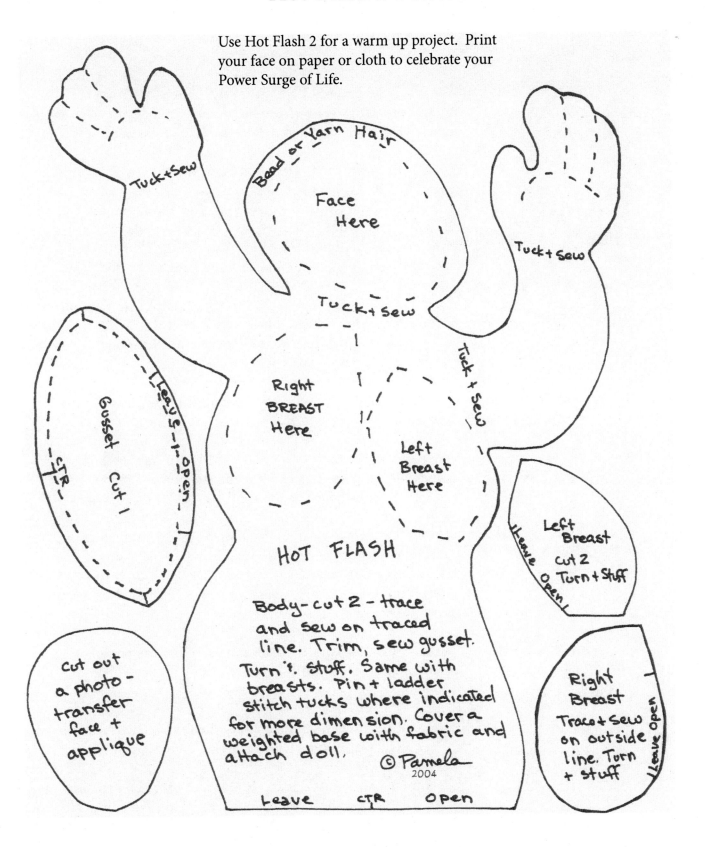

Tuck + Sew

Bead or Yarn Hair

Face Here

Tuck + Sew

Tuck + Sew

Tuck + Sew

Gusset Cut 1

Leave 1 open

CTR

Right BREAST Here

Left Breast Here

Left Breast cut 2 Turn + Stuff

Leave open

HOT FLASH

cut out a photo-transfer face + applique

Body - cut 2 - trace and sew on traced line. Trim, sew gusset. Turn +. Stuff. Same with breasts. Pin + ladder stitch tucks where indicated for more dimension. Cover a weighted base with fabric and attach doll.

© Pamela 2004

Right Breast Trace + sew on outside line. Turn + stuff

Leave open

Leave   CTR   open

Hot Flash Pattern   1

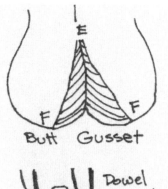

Butt Gusset

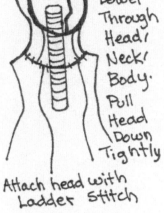

Dowel Through Head/ Neck/ Body. Pull Head Down Tightly

Attach head with Ladder Stitch

Less stuffing

Attach Breast Unit

more stuffing

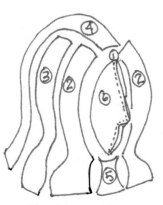

Head Assembly

Making the Original Hot Flash Doll:

These are the pattern pieces from the pattern that was for sale on my website. Copy the pattern pieces and enlarge to make sewing easier. This is a complicated pattern, not for the faint of heart.

Trace pattern pieces on the wrong side of fabric with extra fine Sharpie. Cut the head from unbleached muslin if you want to paint it. Sew the two front pieces together along the profile. Assemble the two side head pieces, being sure that one set is reversed. Join them with the gusset under the chin and the longer one that goes over the top of the head, then insert the face.

Assemble the body parts and stuff, with a dowel sticking out of the neck, pull the head down tightly over the dowel and sew securely, using a ladder stitch. Do a little needle modeling on the face, around the nose and eyebrows before painting the face...use acrylics and follow the diagram on page 60, leave the face plain, or copy a real face, as I did when using this pattern for a Love Yourself doll.

When sewing the two side backs together, insert the butt gusset as shown on the upper left, then add the bottom gusset, with a piece of stiff cardboard and a weight.

The legs are two sides and a back piece that goes against the body, then a sole at the bottom of the foot. The arms are each two pieces with a thumb sewn on at an angle. The breasts have a gusset underneath, then are sewn to the front of the body as shown on the left.

You may want to paint the face and assemble the body before attaching the head to the body.

the hair is a variety of yarns wrapped around a cardboard, sewn across one edge, then clipped across the other edge...or use a copper brillo pad...or anything else that comes to mind.

Use as much stitching, beads, sequins and other embellishments as you can fit onto her nice round body...This Woman is Hot and Proud!

Hot Flash Pattern 2

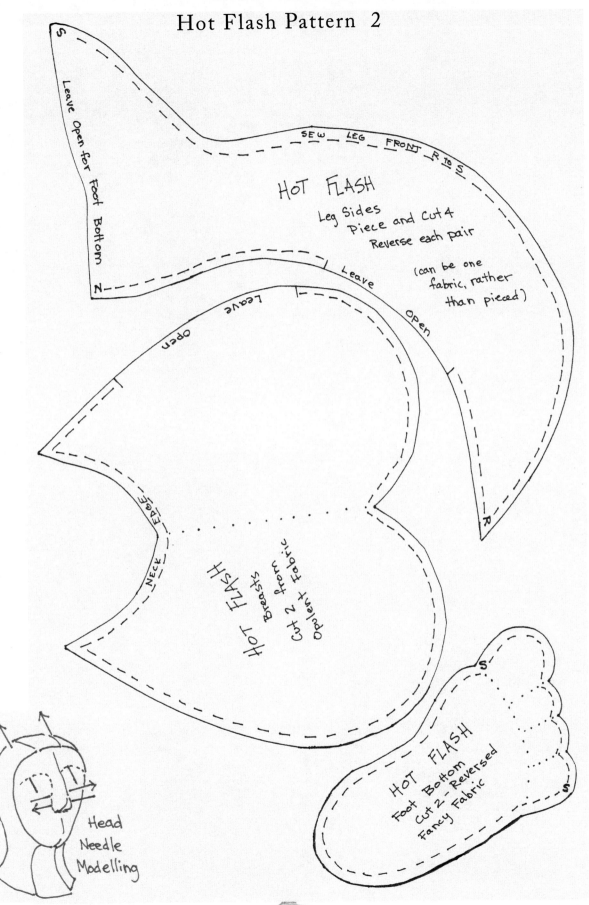

S

Leave Open for Foot Bottom

N

SEW LEG FRONT R TO S

HOT FLASH
Leg Sides
Piece and Cut 4
Reverse each pair

(can be one
fabric, rather
than pieced)

Leave Open

Leave Open

R

NECK EDGE

Hot Flash
Breasts
Cut 2 from
Opulent Fabric

S

HOT FLASH
Foot Bottom
Cut 2 - Reversed
Fancy Fabric

S

Head
Needle
Modelling

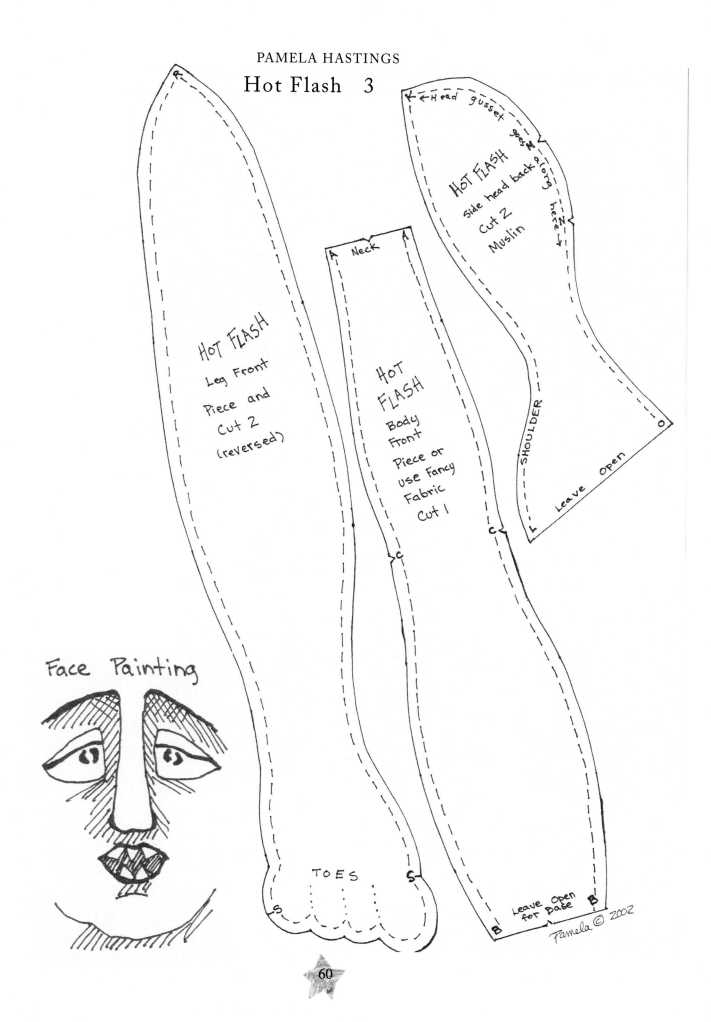

HOT FLASH
Leg Front Piece and Cut 2 (reversed)

Neck

A

HOT FLASH
Body Front Piece or use Fancy Fabric Cut 1

C

TOES

S

← Head gusset goes along here →

HOT FLASH
Side head back
Cut 2 Muslin

SHOULDER

Leave Open

C

B

Leave Open for Base

B

Pamela © 2002

Face Painting

Hot Flash Pattern 4

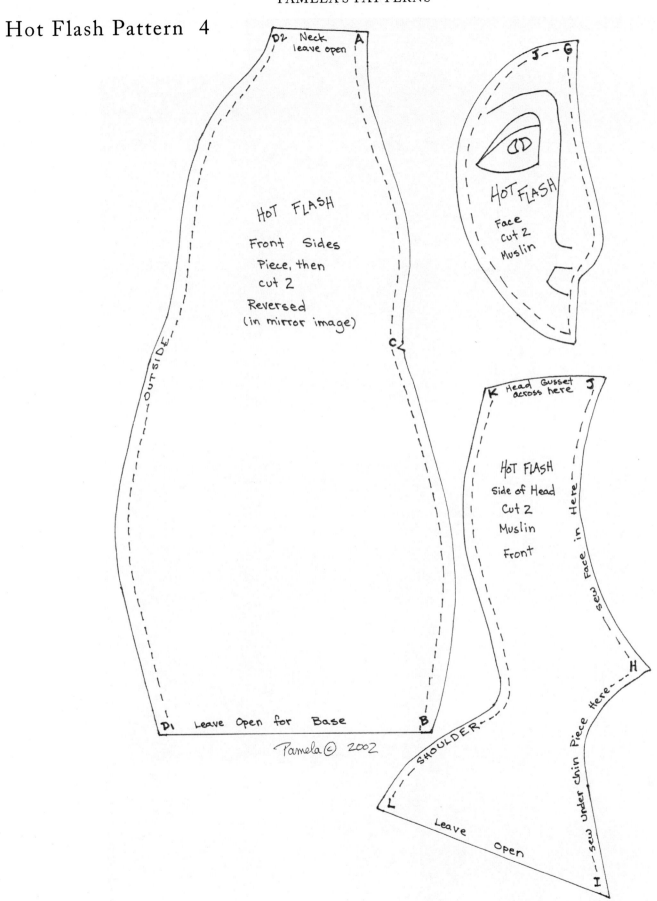

D2 Neck
leave open
A

HOT FLASH

Front Sides
Piece, then
cut 2
Reversed
(in mirror image)

OUTSIDE

C

D1 Leave Open for Base B

Pamela © 2002

J G

HOT FLASH

Face
Cut 2
Muslin

K Head Gusset across here J

HOT FLASH

Side of Head
Cut 2
Muslin

Front

sew Face in Here

sew Under Chin Piece Here

H

L SHOULDER

Leave Open

I

Hot Flash Pattern 5

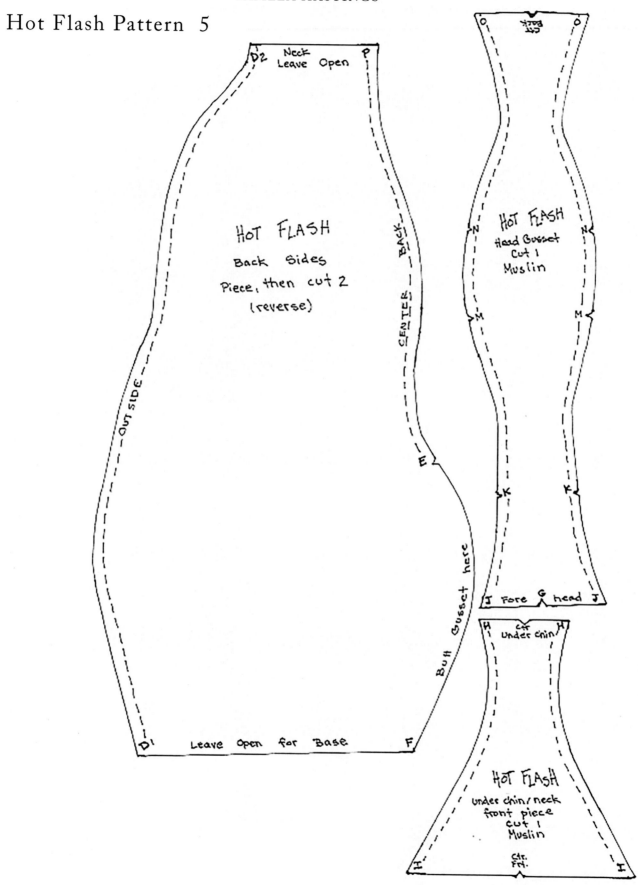

HOT FLASH
Back Sides
Piece, then cut 2
(reverse)

D2 Neck Leave Open P

OUT SIDE

CENTER BACK

Butt Gusset here

E

D1 Leave Open for Base F

HOT FLASH
Head Gusset
Cut 1
Muslin

Cut Back

O O

N N

M M

K K

J Fore G head J

HOT FLASH
Under chin/neck
front piece
cut 1
Muslin

H Ctr Under chin H

H Ctr. Frt. H

Hot Flash 6

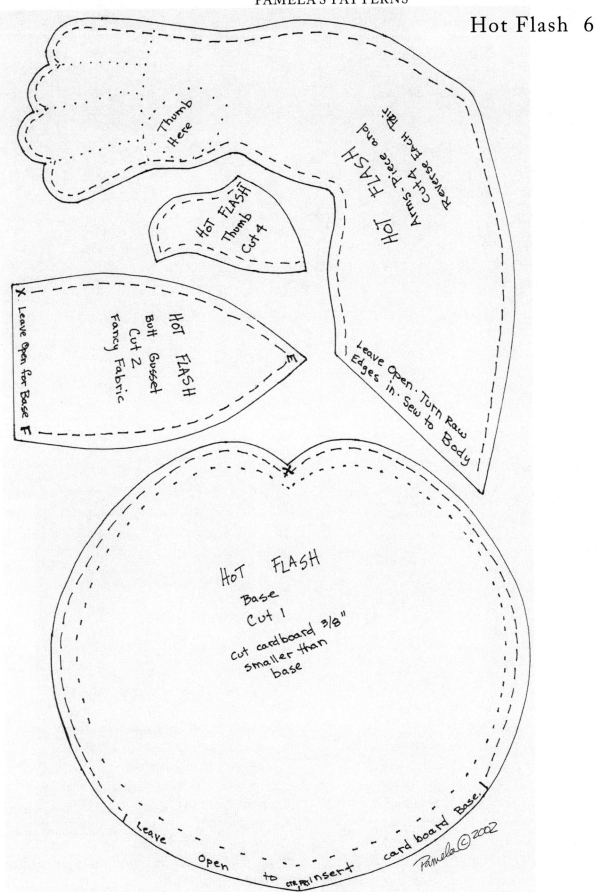

Thumb Here

HoT FLASH
Thumb
Cut 4

HOT FLASH
Arms-Piece and
Cut 4
Reverse Each Fair

Leave Open. Turn Raw
Edges in. Sew to Body

X Leave Open for Base

HoT FLASH
Butt Gusset
Cut 2
Fancy Fabric

HOT FLASH
Base
Cut 1
Cut cardboard 3/8"
smaller than
base

Leave open to ctr. rr. insert cardboard Base.

Pamela © 2002

63

Quilt Block Lion

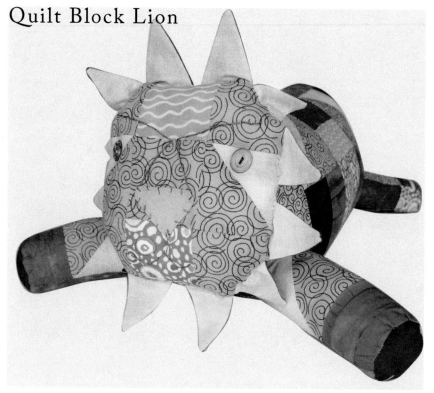

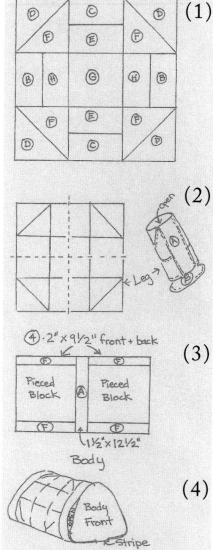

(1)

(2)

(3)

④ · 2" x 9½" front + back

Pieced Block   Ⓐ   Pieced Block

1½" x 12½"

Body

(4)

Body Front

Stripe

Enlarge the pattern

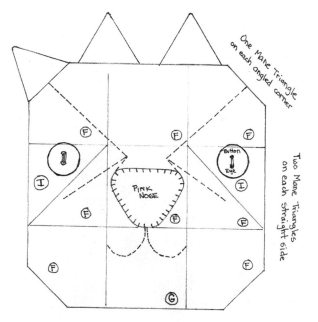

One Mane Triangle on each angled corner

Two Mane Triangles on each straight side

PINK NOSE

Button Eye

Piece the face with 9 blocks as shown above. The two eye blocks are pieced as triangles. Cut out 12 Mane triangles, sew with a different fabric on each side, turn and press without stuffing. The open edge of each triangle is inserted into the seam that attaches the front of the head to the back of the head. trim off the four corners of the face as shown.

Assemble three 9-inch quilt blocks, following diagram (1). Press and square. Cut one of the blocks into quarters to make the legs, with a round paw gusset on the end of each: (2).

Cut the body front and back from color C and back both pieces with iron-on interfacing.

Cut one 1.4" x 12.5" strip from color A, four 2" x 9.5" strips from color F, using these strips with the remaining blocks to create a larger rectangle (3) and assemble the body (4).

Turn and stuff the body, assemble the legs, the head with button eyes and nose, and ladder stitch to the body

Quilt Block Lion

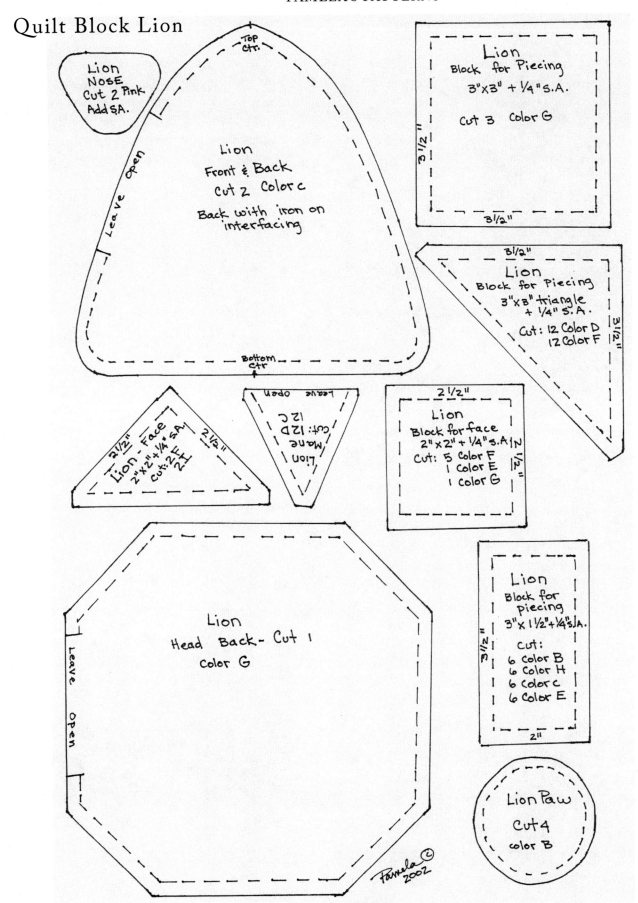

Lion
NOSE
Cut 2 Pink
Add S.A.

TOP CTR.

Leave open

Lion
Front & Back
Cut 2 Color C

Back with iron on interfacing

Bottom ctr

Lion
Block for Piecing
3"x3" + 1/4"S.A.

Cut 3   Color G

3 1/2"

3 1/2"

3 1/2"

Lion
Block for Piecing
3"x3" triangle
+ 1/4" S.A.

Cut: 12 Color D
12 Color F

3 1/2"

Lion - Face
2"x2" + 1/4" S.A.
Cut: 2 F
2 I

2 1/2"

2 1/2"

Leave open

Lion
Mane
Cut: 12 D
12 C

2 1/2"

Lion
Block for face
2"x2" + 1/4"S.A.
Cut: 5 Color F
1 Color E
1 color G

2 1/2"

Lion
Block for
piecing
3"x 1 1/2"+ 1/4"s/A.

Cut:
6 color B
6 color H
6 color C
6 Color E

3 1/2"

2"

Lion
Head Back - Cut 1
Color G

Leave open

Lion Paw
Cut 4
color B

Pamela ©
2002

65

Multi-legged

These two guys grew out of a sketch (below) just for fun, to play with the idea of many legs, the first, at left with a hand-dyed body and head, the second with a pieced body, and the legs attached around the bottom edge of the body so he can sit on the bottom gusset.

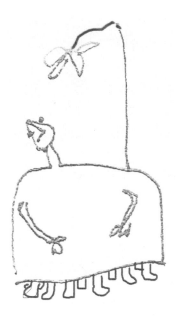

Of course I can never, never stop making new designs and patterns, even though I'm 70. There is NO retirement for artists, and continuing to work/making ART, keeps us engaged and our minds active. I read an article online today that people who keep our minds active are less likely to succumb to the plaques and tangles of Alzheimers' Disease.

Since, like 73% of Americans in 2017, I can't afford residential care in my older age, I suggest that Everyone, follow these patterns and make dolls...or whatever interests you...as a very economical way of staying healthy. Do Doll Making as a Transformative process to stay healthy in body and mind.

Multi-legged Pattern

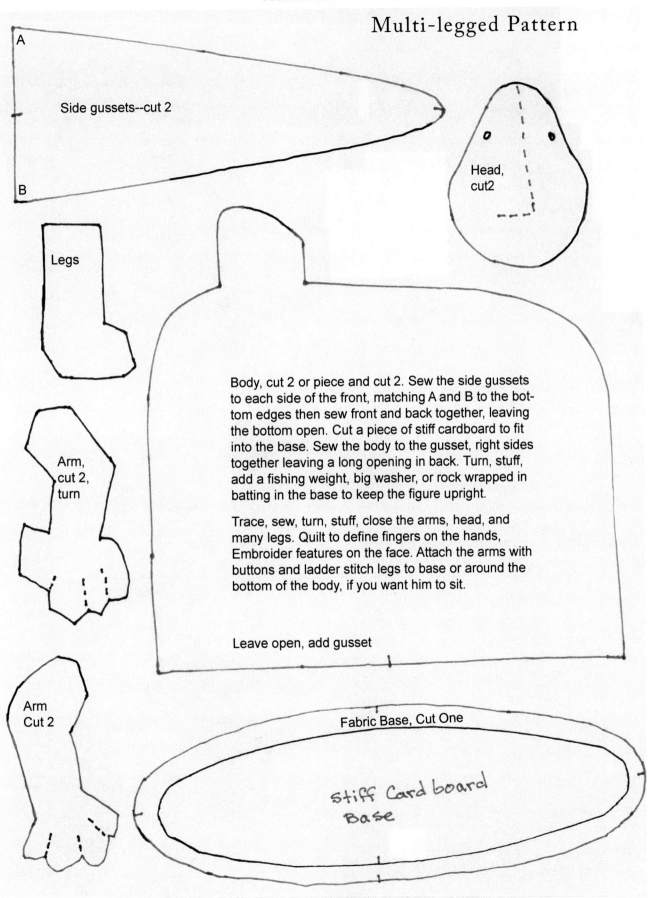

Side gussets--cut 2

A

B

Head, cut2

Legs

Arm, cut 2, turn

Body, cut 2 or piece and cut 2. Sew the side gussets to each side of the front, matching A and B to the bottom edges then sew front and back together, leaving the bottom open. Cut a piece of stiff cardboard to fit into the base. Sew the body to the gusset, right sides together leaving a long opening in back. Turn, stuff, add a fishing weight, big washer, or rock wrapped in batting in the base to keep the figure upright.

Trace, sew, turn, stuff, close the arms, head, and many legs. Quilt to define fingers on the hands, Embroider features on the face. Attach the arms with buttons and ladder stitch legs to base or around the bottom of the body, if you want him to sit.

Leave open, add gusset

Arm Cut 2

Fabric Base, Cut One

Stiff Cardboard Base

Rollers

Two Skaters, simple silhouettes and painted tinker toy wheels, attached with beads on both sides.

On the figure to the left, I painted the muslin body and the wheels with thinned acrylic paints.

For the one below, add the gusset from A to B, ladder stitch the arms on at an angle away from the body for more dimension.

Rollers: The pattern at right is for the lower version, but tinkertoys make fabulous wheels if you want to try the pair above.

Both are made from unbleached muslin, which I recommend for the trial run of any new pattern. I left the single figure plain, because it seemed more expressive that way.

Experiment with tracing figures in motion and then simplify them into your own patterns. In the Eighties, when I was making my living doing craft shows and living in the old schoolhouse in northern Vermont, I made hundreds of dancers and acrobats in muslin, painted simply with acrylics. I even farmed out the stuffing to local young women, paying a quarter a body part.

I painted clouds with rainbows in a wet into wet technique. The 24x36 foot upper schoolroom gave me lots of space to lay out drying parts.

Rolling Pattern

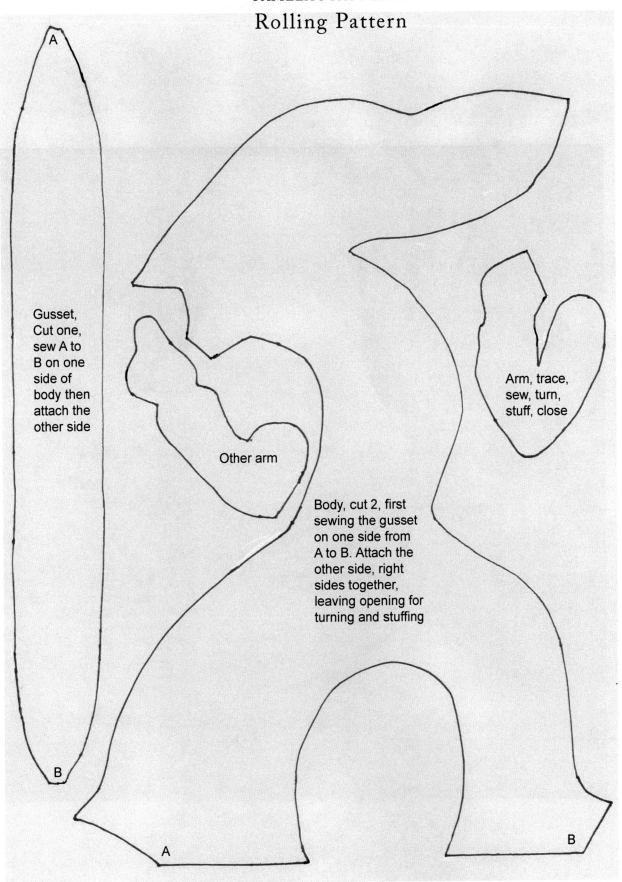

A

Gusset,
Cut one,
sew A to
B on one
side of
body then
attach the
other side

Other arm

Arm, trace,
sew, turn,
stuff, close

Body, cut 2, first
sewing the gusset
on one side from
A to B. Attach the
other side, right
sides together,
leaving opening for
turning and stuffing

B

A

B

Round Heads

I've been having fun playing with cotton scraps and shapes to make a variety of these little guys. Put cardboard and a small weight in the base and they can sit on the edge of a shelf.

Since I first made these in early 2017, my brother, David, dubbed them Pink Hat Protesters. They could be holding signs...or birthday greetings...or whatever you can imagine.

Round Heads Patterns

Gusset, one for each, with a piece of cardboard cut smaller to fit inside and a small weight.

Alternative body. I made the round head size to fit a circle printed on the fabric and pieced the rest to fit. If you draw your body with the same -sized bottom opening, as I've done here, the gusset will fit.
Try one with a big wide head. Have Fun!

Body, piece, trace, sew with right sides together, leaving bottom open for gusset, Quilting between fingers and between ears and head adds dimension.

Attach gusset here

Arms, leave end open for attaching to body

Legs, attach with beads for bending or make long skinny legs

Feather Head

Same pattern, two variations...slight changes in shape, fabric, and embellishment can make a huge difference in the finished piece. Draw around the upper and lower leg pieces together to make one-piece legs. Or just make long, skinny legs as on the left.

As with most of the patterns, trace all pattern pieces on the wrong side, sew with short stitches on the wrong side of the fabric, with right sides together, leaving an opening on a straight edge, turn, stuff, close with ladder stitch.

Use a ladder stitch to attach body parts at right angles.

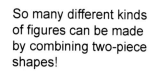

So many different kinds of figures can be made by combining two-piece shapes!

Enlarge this pattern so you won't get frustrated with the many tiny pieces. Trace all parts onto the wrong side of the fabric, two pieces with right sides together. Sew on the traced line, leaving an opening for turning and stuffing. Close the opening with a ladder stitch.

Feather Head

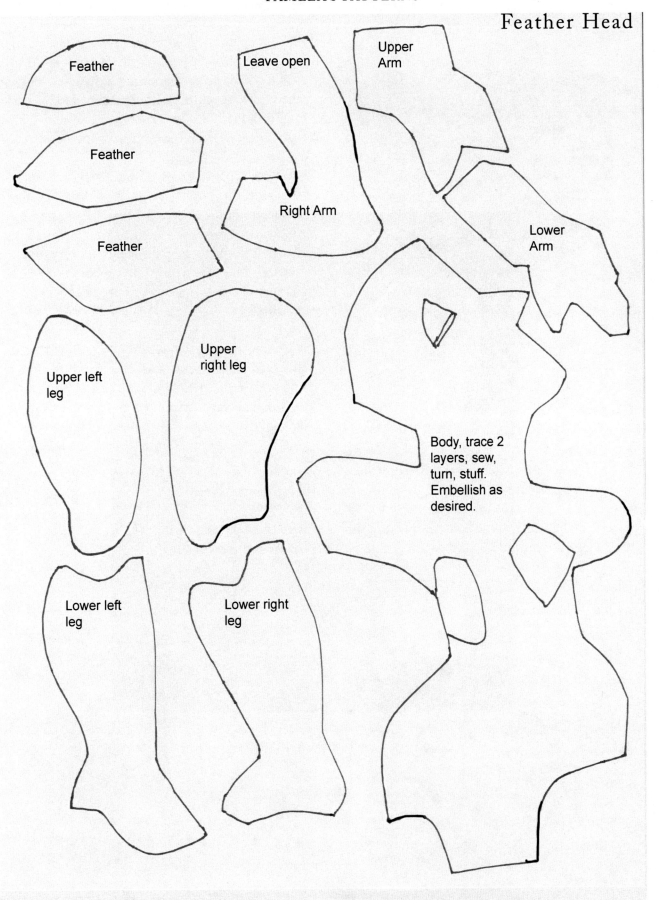

Feather

Feather

Feather

Leave open

Right Arm

Upper
Arm

Lower
Arm

Upper left
leg

Upper
right leg

Body, trace 2
layers, sew,
turn, stuff.
Embellish as
desired.

Lower left
leg

Lower right
leg

I learned pattern making for my own designs by making clothes for myself (gussets and darts), easing one piece to fit another, how shapes change when they are stuffed with a person, and by making Edith Flack Ackley's costume dolls and Women's Day patterns in the Sixties for toy dolls.

I collected costume ideas from paper dolls and magazines and kept steno pads of ideas. My maternal grandmother was my first, best customer AND taught me to sew with a thimble. My mother encouraged me to keep drawings of every doll I made. A nice lady from Chicago bought my little girl costume dolls for $5 each to sell at her church bazaar.

A person wanting to buy something I made was always the ultimate compliment, from the time I sold grab bags I made in grade school, to a commissioned soft sculpture of Lee Iacocca in one of his cars that appeared with him in Time Magazine.

Now mostly it's nice to have someone love one of my pieces enough to want to take it home and display it...although money is still much appreciated.

Whatever your reasons for making things, I hope these patterns bring you joy...and lots of new ideas for designing your own variations and creating new creatures.

Felt Friends, pattern p. 38

Resources

pamela@pamelahastings.com...email me with any questions

https://www.pamelahastings.com/

https://pamelabythesea.wordpress.com/ My blog for current work, patterns, thoughts

www.facebook.com/pamela.hastings.73

Designing a Doll and Making Faces Book, Pamela Hastings...available from the Author

Amazon page for my Kindle books and Printing on Demand books: www.amazon.com/Pamela_Hastings/e/BO1FZQ8LXG

Watch the video on how to design a gusset on my channel: youtube/user/pamelahastings1

Jo-Ann's or any fabric store for unbleached muslin, batting, Polyfil stuffing, threads, embellishments
www.dharmatrading.com for printable fabric or Jo-Ann's
Any acrylic paints or fabric markers--experiment on a scrap first
Use light-weight interfacing to stabilize any fabric that might be stretchy
Stuff more firmly than you think you need to, in order to maintain the shape over time.

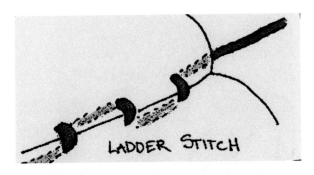

LADDER STITCH

Ladder Stitch: Pin the edges of the opening or the parts to be attached close together with long quilting pins. Run the needle/thread inside the fold on one side, straight across to the fold on the other side, working back and forth and trying to keep the thread as invisible as possible.

Create Icon...use any icon pattern.

Made in the USA
Columbia, SC
12 December 2021

51149096R00044